From unpaid stagehand to calypso singer to screen star par excellence, the inspirational career of Harry Belafonte shines forth as *the* modern edifice to the black man's will to create and succeed in the crucible of racial discrimination and professional antagonism. During his dynamic career Belafonte has been called King of Calypso, balladeer, blues singer, matinee idol, dramatic actor of stage and screen and movie mogul. But the goal of the real Belafonte has always been to avoid being pinned down and stereotyped. His life force continues to drive him from one creative project to another, leaving in his wake a world changed for the better by the magic Belafonte touch. He may deny being the King of Claypso, but he'll understand when we call him Lord Harry, The Actor.

BELAFONTE

BELAFONTE

BY GENIA FOGELSON

AN ORIGINAL HOLLOWAY HOUSE EDITION
HOLLOWAY HOUSE PUBLISHING CO.
LOS ANGELES, CALIFORNIA

PUBLISHED BY
Holloway House Publishing Company
8060 Melrose Avenue
Los Angeles, California 90046
All rights reserved. No part of this book may be reproduced or transmitted in any form or by any means, electronic or mechanical, including photocopying, recording or by any information storage and retrieval system, without permission in writing from the Publisher. Copyright © 1980 by Hollywood House Publishing Company. Any similarity to persons living or dead is purely coincidental.
International Standard Book Number 0-87067-680-6
Printed in the United States of America
Cover illustration by Jesse Santos
Cover design by Davidson Graphics

CONTENTS

CHAPTER ONE
Harlem to Kingston to Harlem — 13

CHAPTER TWO
Performer, Husband, Father — 23

CHAPTER THREE
The Folk Singer — 39

CHAPTER FOUR
The Ascending Star — 53

CHAPTER FIVE
Bittersweet Success — 69

CHAPTER SIX
Crucial Times — 81

CHAPTER SEVEN
A Divorce and A Marriage — 97

CHAPTER EIGHT
King of Calypso 113

CHAPTER NINE
From Surgery to Stardom 129

CHAPTER TEN
The Moviemaker 145

CHAPTER ELEVEN
Harry the Man 163

CHAPTER TWELVE
The Powerful Years 175

CHAPTER THIRTEEN
Lord Harry, The Actor 193

DISCOGRAPHY 209

FILMOGRAPHY 213

ABOUT THE AUTHOR 215

To Norman

To Professor Noakes

BELAFONTE

Chapter One
Harlem to Kingston to Harlem

Because of his songs, many people think that Harry Belafonte was born in the West Indies. However, although he lived in Kingston, Jamaica, for several years as a youth, he was actually born in Harlem in a hospital on East 70th Street on March 1, 1927. Baptized Harold George Belafonte, he was Roman Catholic. His father, Harold George Belafonte, Sr., was a cook in the British Royal Navy. His mother, Melvine Love Belafonte, was a domestic servant and a dressmaker.

Both of Harry's parents were from the West Indies, and both of them had one white parent. Belafonte Sr., from Martinique (F.W.I.), gave up his French citizenship during World War I to become a British subject. Melvine Love Belafonte was from Jamaica (B.W.I.). Harry's maternal grandmother and his paternal grandfather were both white.

Harry Belafonte as a youth had a lot of hostility. There are several reasons why he felt great frustration and anger. One was because he was a black being raised in an area of Harlem that was mostly white. In order to get to school—P.S. 186 at 145th Street and Amsterdam Avenue—he had to walk several blocks through a mainly white neighborhood, exposed to teasing and bullying. Another possible reason for his hostility was the fact that his family was poor. When Harry's father was not shipping out as a chef, they were often on relief. And before young Belafonte was six, his father sailed off for good with a white woman.

Not only, then, did young Harry have to endure poverty and racial discrimination, he also had other problems related to his father. Harry Belafonte, Sr., was not nice to his wife when he was at home, and to make matters worse, his father preferred his younger son, Dennis, to Harry because Dennis had lighter skin. Being a West Indian, his father had marked caste ideas. "White" characteristics, such as light eyes, light skin and soft hair, were thought of as superior to more "Negro" ones. As Dennis looked "whiter" than Harry, his father preferred him. Young Harry, then, felt the pain and discrimination of his blackness even in his own family.

If Harry has had trouble indentifying with his own people, as has been said, it is easy to see that discrimination among his schoolmates and within his own family could have created the difficulty.

The fact that Harry did not have a father to raise him created a permanent void. Later, Harry often tried to find father substitutes in older men. Fortunately, his mother raised him with dignity and care. She instilled in him a determination in the face of adversity which was of great value to Harry in his later years. She taught him to struggle and to always hope for something better. She is known to be a very proud woman, and she taught Harry to walk with pride and dignity. Described as being rather touchy, she was not hostile, just wary of whites. Harry's mother, in spite of her bouts with poverty and her own difficulties, fought hard to give her children everything she could.

In school, the interracial tensions were felt by young Belafonte. He had to fight about children's nursey rhymes ("Eeny, meeny, miny, mo") and other such things which took place between races at school. He was sometimes involved in street gangs who fought each other. Harry's mother was often called to her son's school to talk about Harry's behavior. He was a disciplinary problem because he was often bored in class. Perhaps the fact that he had a good mind, too good for his school, partly explains his boredom and unruly behavior.

Because of the dangers of bringing up her sons in the tough, crime-ridden streets of Harlem, and also on account of Harry's poor behavior at school, his mother took Harry and Dennis to Jamaica. She had decided to complete their schooling in Kingston. In the streets of Harlem, Harry was hit by a car while chasing a ball into the street. Right before that, he'd fallen on a pair of shears and injured one eye. His mother hoped that Kingston would provide a less hazardous environment in which her sons could finish school in peace.

Harry was nine when he started school in Jamaica.

One would think that in beautiful Jamaica the problems of living would be lessened. However, Harry, already a troubled, belligerent boy, only found different problems with which to contend. For one thing, among his relatives in the West Indies there was still the shade of his skin to place him in the lower ranks. His relatives had the same attitude toward the value of light skin and eyes that his father had. So Harry was held in low esteem even by his own flesh and blood.

Another problem for young Belafonte in Jamaica was the fact that he was used to American ways, while his schoolmates were British with different customs. This made Harry feel different. And Harry wasn't used to wearing shorts to school. In fact, the whole British tradition was foreign to the boy from Harlem, and again there were fights and arguments.

Perhaps the biggest difficulty for the already troubled young Harry was his new loneliness, brought about by the fact that in Jamaica he went to various boarding schools. Amid unfamiliar surroundings, feeling strange among all the British students and not held in high regard by his own relatives because of his color, Harry became lonely and "difficult" in school. Rather than listen in class, he began to dream of becoming someone outstanding. In his troubled, unhappy head he wanted to do something that would break down the barriers so he would be accepted by everyone. It is said that he wanted to become a jockey, even tried to stunt his growth, but he was soon too tall. It was perhaps during those lonely years in Kingston that he started looking around for a career that would answer his prayers.

Although Harry's years in Jamaica were no happier

than his earlier ones in Harlem, there was one thing about Kingston that was essential to his development as a singer—the local music. The young Belafonte heard the crazy, strangely accented songs of the calypso singers in the streets of Kingston. It is said that Kingston is an environment that sings. The peddlers and other people of business and even politics all sing in the streets. Not only was the calypso music to prove important to Harry's singing career, but the warm atmosphere of Kingston might account in part for some of the warmth in Belafonte's songs.

Harry's stay in Kingston was not all unpleasant. In spite of his personal difficulties, he enjoyed the beauty of the endless beaches and the taste of the ripe fruit. There was an atmosphere of peacefulness and freedom in Jamaica, with its flowers and warm nights, that didn't exist in cold, dirty Harlem.

Harry's mother, by then Mrs. Writht, came back to get her son when he was thirteen. Probably she thought he could get a better education and more easily find work in the States. Soon, Harry was again living in a mostly white neighborhood.

Racial prejudice was rife in Harlem. In this predominantly Irish and Spanish neighborhood, Harry once again entered the New York school system. It is said that Harry and his brother tried alternately to pass for Greeks, or as natives from Martinique. The only trouble with "passing" for white was that you had to listen to the racial jokes in silence. But Harry has always had fierce racial pride. He was soon angered over something someone said and the fights started again.

Harry was the kind of young man who lashed out if

someone said something he didn't like. Although he didn't use dangerous weapons such as knives, he did sustain many an injury from fighting in the streets of Harlem. However, the emotional scars were more lasting than the physical ones. Although he was accepted on sports teams by his classmates because of his physical abilities, he was excluded from all social activities because he was black. In his early years as a superstar it was probably the violence, the hostility just beneath the surface of his handsome face and gentle singing that made him interesting and exciting.

If Jamaica, with its songs and its beauty, was important to Belafonte's career, so was Harlem, with its racial traumas, its frustrations, its poverty, and Harry's violent, angry reacton to it all.

In his second year of high school, Harry was getting more and more angry at the situations around him. He was attending George Washington High in the Bronx—supposedly because a girl he liked was a student there—but the prejudice and meaninglessness of the classes still exasperated him. The things he was asked to learn did not help him with his own unhappy life, and they certainly didn't change the terrible slums of Harlem. Harry hated having to fight with people constantly just to be considered a human being. He despised being humiliated because of the color of his skin.

At this stage in his life, Harry had no sense of identity. He still did not know what direction to take in order to escape the life he lived. Although his mother loved him, the loneliness he felt at being alienated from the world, as he saw it, was unbearable. The years he'd spent in Jamaica had only made him feel more removed from people.

By his second year of high school, Harry was feeling estranged, a victim of his poverty and his blackness. The Navy offered him a chance to escape his deplorable situation. In 1944, people were joining together to fight the enemy. Blacks were being allowed to join the services, and Harry was suddenly caught up in the surge of patriotism that was sweeping the country. There was a unity and a togetherness about serving in the armed forces. Here was a chance to fight dictatorship and racial hatred. In order to escape his own unhappiness, Belafonte joined the Navy, not bothering to complete high school.

He was allowed to attend the Navy's Storekeeper School at Hampton, Virginia, because he'd scored high in the IQ test. Here he was to learn even more about the injustices leveled at blacks, as the southern Negro was even more ostracized from society than the blacks of Harlem. Harry became involved in long, heated discussions among the northern and southern blacks in his unit. It seemed that in Virginia, discrimination was an accepted thing. At least in Harlem, in spite of the constant gang wars, there was some integration. In later years, while touring as a singer and an actor, Harry Belafonte was to encounter first-hand racial prejudice in the South.

Although there was some unpleasantness associated with being a black stationed in Virginia, Belafonte gained a great deal from his tour in the Navy. He began to enlarge his vision of the world, to become aware that there was more than poverty, loneliness and basic survival available to him. He made friends, began to read and learned a lot in discussions with his fellow servicemen. People talked about who they were and where they were going, and Harry started to form an identity.

Not only did Belafonte open his vistas to the world while in the Navy, but he also met his first wife, Margurite. In 1944, Frances Margurite Byrd was a student at Hampton Institute in Newport News, Virginia. Harry was training with a Navy unit at Hampton, trying to become a Navy storekeeper. As the girls college was playing host to the servicemen stationed at the far end of their campus, social privileges were exchanged.

It seems that Margurite, a senior studying to be a child psychologist, was against socializing with servicemen. She led a delegation to the president's office to protest the presence of the "gobs."

The first meeting between Harry and the proud Margurite took place when she was officiating at a freshman garden party on the lawn of the president's home. The servicemen, not far away from the festivities, began to heckle the girls. Harry, hooting louder than the rest at the authority and sham of the tea party, drew her attention.

Harry must have been attracted to Margurite, for he followed her home. When he asked her for a date she refused, saying that she didn't make dates with sailors. It's reported that at this point young Belafonte told Margurite she'd better be nice to him. When she asked "Why?" he replied:

"Because one of these days I'm going to end up being your husband."

It took Belafonte some time to convince the proud

senior to go out with him. However, when they did start seeing each other, a whole new world was opened for Harry. They had endless discussions about racial issues, about life. Margurite was from a secure, middle-class black family. Her father was in real estate and her family was an educated one. All of her sisters and brothers went to college and became teachers. Margurite, herself, was to later study in France and Germany and ultimately to receive her Ph.D. from New York University.

Margurite had been raised in a black world, with no problems of integration or racial prejudice to dim her self-esteem. She lived in Washington, D.C., in a comfortable, stable, segregated community, and she'd attended all-black schools. She had all the clothes she wanted, and her family, when she was growing up, went to the zoo, to movies, to baseball games.

She was to see how different her life had been to Harry's. Margurite had been isolated from the worries that had plagued Belafonte on the fierce streets of Harlem, and she wasn't dependent in any way on white people. She was amazed, shocked by Harry's stormy, hostile personality. She was calm, with a strong sense of identity, whereas he was tense, insecure, quick-tempered and belligerent. As she talked with him she realized he had storms rampaging inside him—he was searching for a direction, he was uncertain about his future, and he was hurt, resentful and really angry about being black and not accepted.

Margurite was secure in her blackness. As she was also well read, she gave Harry some perspective on the way the Negro's position was shifting in America and in the world. She urged him to read books on Negro art, history and culture.

It is said that Harry and Margurite clashed constantly because he was explosive and hostile to the world around him, and she was comfortable and accepting. However, Harry admired Margurite and she, even though she kept him at a distance, was much taken with him. Writers and researchers of later years have pointed out that perhaps the relationship between Margurite and Harry was in many ways like that of a mother and son, or even psychologically, like father and son. Harry did not have the strong, firm upbringing that enabled him to have pride in himself and an identity. He was always searching for strength in people to replace that childhood lack.

Whatever the relationship was, she was strong and had the self-confidence that was supportive to Harry in his early years as a struggling entertainer. Even though they met in 1944, they were not married until 1948. At Christmas time in 1944, Harry completed his Storekeeper's course and was given orders to report to the West Coast for possible active duty in the Pacific. He gave her a few presents and they said goodbye for the time being.

In 1945 Harry was honorably discharged from the Navy without seeing overseas duty. He began working as a maintenance man in New York City. In 1946 he would begin seeing Margurite again. Things would be different at this point: she would be a graduate student at New York University and he would be a young man with a burning desire to become an actor.

Chapter Two
Performer, Husband, Father

The years 1945 through 1949 were crucial ones for Harry Belafonte. He decided that what he wanted to be in life was an actor. During those years he began to succeed in a sister art—singing. And during those years of struggle he also became a husband and a father.

Harry saw his first play in December of 1945. He'd been employed as a maintenance man in Harlem by his stepfather after his discharge from the Navy. One of the tenants in an apartment in which Harry worked gave him two tickets to a theater production. Belafonte loved movies, but he'd never seen a play. The play, *Home is the Hunter*, by Samuel M. Kootz, was presented by the American Negro Theater in a Harlem playhouse.

Belafonte was absolutely transfixed by the play. It was not the play, which only ran one night and was not successful; it was the acting, the *theater*, that turned the young man on. It is said that he thought about nothing but the play, saw his name in lights for days and nights afterwards. He imagined it was himself on stage, a *somebody*. The audiences were cheering him. Harry Belafonte was stagestruck from this point on.

Harry wanted to become an actor. Not knowing exactly how to become one, he started hanging around the American Negro Theater (ANT). Before he knew it, he was a volunteer stagehand. When he was not doing his maintenance jobs, he moved scenery, painted, strung cables. More than the work of stagehand, he was around a world that was thrilling to him, being among actors and directors.

The director of the ANT soon noticed Harry, who even though he was too thin, was very good looking. He was given a small part in a play. Even though he was shy and had fears and doubts about acting, he went through with the part. Next he was assigned the juvenile lead in a comedy about Harlem, *On Striver's Row*. Both the cast and the director saw Harry's unmistakable personal magnetism, even though he was untrained and inexperienced.

Belafonte, a perfectionist when there was something he really wanted to do, decided to study acting in order to be a successful actor. He found out that there was a dramatic workshop run by Erwin Piscator, a well-known German director. This drama workshop was associated with the New School for Social Research on 12th Street in Manhattan, and it accepted students under the GI Bill of Rights. Since Harry was eligible for benefits, he enrolled.

Performer, Husband, Father

This must have been a time of decision for Harry, for at the time he enrolled in acting classes he also moved away from home. Leaving Harlem, he found a place with some other acting students in Greenwich Village, a haven for creative people, bohemians and striving artists. Their apartment was on Bleeker Street. Not only was this a time of physical moving away from home and Harlem, but it was also a psychological and cultural rupture. Belafonte began educating himself; he read about music and culture and became involved in the arts and literature. As it happens with so many talented, creative people who get a false start in school, all of the things that Harry refused to learn in school became fascinating to him.

Education became vital and exciting. His desire to become an actor started his creativity and intellect flowing, and these years were exciting to him, in spite of the hardships of looking for acting work.

In one article on Belafonte's time as an acting student, it's pointed out that one reason why he didn't stand out as exceptional was because he had some very stiff competition. In his class was Marlon Brando, who would be soon starring on Broadway (*A Streetcar Named Desire*). Also studying with him were Tony Curtis and Sidney Poitier.

The name of Poitier weaves in and out of the story of Belafonte. They are approximately the same age and both were born in big cities (Miami for Sidney) while being from the Islands (Poitier is from the Bahamas). Poitier also went back to the Islands to school, again returning to face racial strife in his high school years. Both began acting at the American Negro Theater and both ended up studying acting at the same time. In some of the later chapters it will be discussed how they collaborated in films as actors, producers and directors, both sharing convictions that it was up to the black man to make films about black people that were meaningful.

However, at the time of their studying in school, Belafonte was a poor young man with a dream and a Village apartment costing him $9.50 a month. Poitier was struggling with a thick Bahamian accent that was making it difficult for him to get work.

Belafonte had less training than some of the students and he was shy. However, he had determination and drive. He worked very hard, read all the time and participated in the workshop projects. While he was at the workshop, Harry appeared in some of their musicals. In one production Belafonte did two numbers, "Recognition," which he wrote himself, and "Lean On Me."

Monte Kay, who was at the time an aspiring producer, heard Belafonte sing and was impressed. He even went up to the young acting student after the performance and promised him work when he, Monte, got a job as a producer. There was something about Harry, even though he had no training as a singer, that was impressive. Harry told Monte Kay that he wanted to act, not sing.

As fate would have it, in January of 1949, just before Belafonte was to give up the arts in order to take a job and support his family, he stumbled into Monte Kay's jazz night club and before the night was out was given a singing contract. Monte Kay was also to become his first agent.

Performer, Husband, Father

However, before this lucky break, Belafonte spent several years pounding the streets in search of acting jobs, without success. He also, during the years from his acting lessons until his breakthrough in Kay's nightclub, started seeing Margurite Byrd again, married her and awaited the birth of his daughter Adrienne.

Margurite and Harry had written letters to each other while he was in the service and she was doing graduate work. He appeared on her doorstep, after not having seen her in two years, in 1946. She was still at home, in Washington, D.C., getting ready to move to New York to attend New York University. Harry was in Washington with a protest group which was marching on the White House with a petition.

She was glad to know that while she was studying in New York there would be someone there she knew. At this time Margurite did not consider Harry seriously as a future mate, but she liked him as a person. During the years she studied at NYU and later taught school, while Belafonte struggled to make it as an actor, they saw each other.

Margurite noticed that Harry's racial hostility was still strong. One of his pastimes while riding the subway was to scrawl comments on the advertising posters which, to him, showed racial prejudice. On the ads which promised that if you used their lotion you would always have soft, white hands, he wrote, "What about black hands?" Margurite thought this was childish and would only result in possible arrest. She told him he was not speaking out as he thought, but merely letting off steam. Margurite told him that he must grow within himself, make himself important enough to be heard.

Harry's counter to this brought up another bone of contention between them. He replied that it was hard to become important when he couldn't even get a decent role as an actor. To Margurite, that was part of the problem. Being, or rather trying to be, an actor was a dead-end situation. She was from a middle-class family where people had nine-to-five jobs. Harry should be preparing himself for one of the professions, rather than trying to make it in an area that was almost impossible for a Negro.

There just weren't enough roles for black people in theater. Also, the bohemians in the Village that Harry hung around with were not her type.

However, in spite of their differences, they continued to see each other. Perhaps Margurite wanted to change Harry. Certainly she represented strength and achievement to him. She was attracted by the big kid in him, the child who lashes out and writes on signs in subways and needs protecting. He saw her as a rock while everything else in his world was uncertain. It was the middle-class in her, the fact that she knew where she was going, that made him care for her, even though as an artist he rebelled against the middle class and its mores. It is said that from their first encounter, through those years in New York City, he told her they were getting married.

Finally, one evening in 1948, he invited her to a play in which he was acting. After the play he asked her to marry him, and she accepted. This particular play had been impressive even to Margurite, who usually didn't enjoy watching Harry's performances. It was an off-Broadway production, *Sojourner Truth,* based on the exploits of the Negro woman abolitionist who fought

Performer, Husband, Father

slavery in the days of the underground railroad. Harry played her son and was quite good. Margurite decided that she really did want to be Mrs. Belafonte, and they were married in a civil ceremony on Friday, June 18, 1948.

Their first summer together was spent traveling from one place to another. Harry was on the entertainment staff of a summer camp at Beaver Lodge in Pennsylvania, and Margurite was teaching in Manhattan. They got together on weekends.

In the fall, the problem of Harry's finding work again became an issue. Margurite was making seventy-five dollars a week teaching and Harry was earning nothing, as he was looking for acting work. He visited producers' offices, registered with agents, went to plays in rehearsal, but generally there weren't many jobs available for Negro actors. Mostly, it was a fruitless, frustrating search. There were plays about blacks even in the Forty's, or at least plays with blacks as characters. There was Philip Yordan's *Anna Lucasta* and a few others. However, for an unknown actor like Belafonte, the opportunities were too rare to be worthwhile.

He became frustrated and unhappy. Margurite was, by December of 1948, in her fifth month of pregnancy, and she did not consider Harry's desire to become an actor very realistic. It was decided that Margurite would return home to Washington for the rest of her pregnancy and the birth of their baby. Harry would look for work.

For the next month Belafonte wandered around Broadway. His acting school buddy, Brando, was by this time starring in a Broadway production, *A Streetcar*

Named Desire. However, Harry's other friend from drama school, Sidney Poitier, was working in the garment district. He, too, wanted to succeed as an actor, but he worked in order to pay the rent.

Belafonte did some work in the garment district, but at the last minute, before taking a full time job and perhaps giving up his dream of becoming an actor, he landed his first singing engagement. Monte Kay offered him seventy dollars a week, and after his first week he was asked to stay for nineteen weeks. So Harry was able to call his wife and tell her he'd found work. He was able to afford a New York apartment for his wife and baby-to-be. In June Margurite moved back to New York, and in September the couple moved their daughter Adrienne into their first apartment.

The night Belafonte stumbled into the Royal Roost, he'd probably been walking around Broadway as usual, looking at the theater lights. The Roost, located between 47th and 48th Streets on the west side of Broadway, was a midtown jazz club. The club sponsored a new type of jazz coming out of Harlem. When Harry descended the stairs to the club, he saw Monte Kay, the producer he'd met while an acting student.

As mentioned earlier, Kay turned out to be one of the club's managers. The Roost had a policy of allowing aspiring jazz singers to try out for a week's booking. Monte Kay asked Harry to sing a few songs. Harry was surprised, but went on the stage and sang the two numbers from his acting class musical, "Lean on Me" and "Recognition." Kay recognized that same magical quality that had captured his attention the first time he'd heard Belafonte sing the two songs. "Recognition," which Harry had written, was about the frustration he felt as a Negro being deprived of recognition as a man. Perhaps some of the anger and hostility that gave Belafonte's performances such vigor was visible when Harry sang this song. Whatever it was, Kay saw enough promise in the young man to offer him a week's contract at seventy dollars.

Harry was stunned, as he wasn't looking for work as a singer. However, it had to be better than pushing a cart in the garment district. It was also a Broadway night club.

Kay felt that the audience liked young Belafonte. He was inexperienced, awkward and too thin, but he had magic. The week's engagement stretched to twenty weeks, and Monte Kay became Harry's first manager.

During this time Belafonte appeared at Carnegie Hall, as one of many performers in a jazz concert. It was strange, for although he had decided that his salvation in life would come if he could be accepted as an actor, Belafonte as a jazz singer received an award from the Negro newspaper *The Pittsburgh Courier* as "the vocal find of the year."

He was groomed by his manager as a Billy Eckstine type of jazz singer, and later as a pop singer. Belafonte cut his first commercial record while at the Roost, his song "Recognition" with "Lean on Me" on the other side. It is reported that 10,000 copies were sold in New York, but the local record company didn't market the song out of the area.

Belafonte got excellent training while at the Roost, which featured such talented musicians as Charlie "Bird" Parker, Miles Davis and Dizzy Gillespie. Their accompaniment to his singing presented daring, experimental jazz which forced him to compete with vocal gymnastics in order to be heard.

When his twenty weeks were over, Monte Kay got other bookings for Harry as a jazz or pop singer. For about two years Belafonte traveled and pursued his singing career. Finally, after this period of time, even though he was making good money and was liked as a jazz and pop singer, Belafonte decided this was not what he wanted to do, and he walked out on an engagement in Miami.

People who look back on Belafonte's brief period as a pop/jazz singer say he took the jobs, even though he didn't like the kind of singing he had to do, because he thought the singing might somehow lead to acting jobs. What Harry objected to particularly about pop singing was the lyrics. He didn't like the insincerity, the silliness of jazz and pop lyrics, so he didn't really put himself into the singing. However, as a folk singer, Belafonte is emotional, stunning, because he believes in what he's singing.

During these few years a few things happened in Belafonte's career, but they mostly led to dead ends. He was given a record contract by Capitol Records. He sang some pop songs, including "How Green Was My Valley," and "They Didn't Believe Me." His style seemed to critics to be a combination of Frank Sinatra's slowness and Billy Eckstine's vibrato heaviness. He wasn't very original, as he was at this point trying to find a style. Six months later, on December 20, 1949, he recorded four more songs for Capitol, including "Farewell to Arms" and "Sometimes I Feel Like a Motherless

Child." There was little enthusiasm for his recordings, and his contract was not renewed.

Belafonte and his friend Sidney Poitier attempted to form a comedy team. They rehearsed together for awhile on the roof of Harry's building on 156th Street, but they decided soon that neither one of them was cut out for comedy. They'd been friends for a while, even sharing unemployment checks and theater tickets when money was scarce. Neither one had made it as an actor at this point; Harry didn't count his singing engagements as successes, first of all because he wasn't acting, and second, because he didn't like the kind of singing he was doing.

When his new manager Monte Kay saw that Harry was doing well at the Royal Roost, he started booking his client into other spots. Kay was asked to produce a show for a new night spot, Birdland. Birdland, which became the mecca of jazz fans all over the world, was named for Charley "Bird" Parker, the alto saxophonist who would become one of the most notable figures in modern jazz. At the time when Harry was asked to sing, Kay presented a two hour show telling the growth of jazz from New Orleans Dixieland to New York pop. Belafonte sang some jazz songs as part of the cavalcade. In the reviews he was not praised particularly. For example, *Variety* wrote, "On vocals Belafonte is okay, if not particularly standout on a brace of romantic ballads."

During this period and the next year, Kay was able to book Belafonte into some New York clubs and several out-of-town places. He was not fantastically successful, nor was he very happy during this period, as he was not singing anything which interested him. There was a booking for over a month at Cafe Society Downtown, in Greenwich Village.

This time *Variety* gave him better notices, perhaps because the pop he was singing was at least more to his liking than the jazz he did at Birdland. *Variety* wrote that Belafonte handled ballads with sensitivity, and concluded that he was "still a vocalist of promise." Another critic noticed improvement in Belafonte since he switched from his "Recognition" song to more standard ones. However, Harry was by no means considered a challenge to Billy Eckstine.

Although Monte Kay and Virginia Wicks, Harry's other manager, continued to book Belafonte into various clubs, they knew that he hadn't found himself, nor was he committed to what he was doing. He functioned as a jazz and pop singer merely because he found this the most practical way to try to get into acting. His singing lacked intensity and emotion because he didn't feel anything for it. Later his folk singing would be thrilling because of the color and heat he gave to it.

At the time Belafonte was singing jazz and pop he made it known that he thought the lyrics were not believable. Most singers didn't think much about lyrics, as jazz was so intricate that the words weren't really important. However, Harry did express his feelings that the songs sounded phony. When he later got into folk singing, Belafonte became very conscious of the words he sang, spending time looking for songs that meant something to him.

His dissatisfaction with his career culminated on Christmas of 1959. On that night, Belafonte walked out

Performer, Husband, Father

of a club in Miami, Martha Raye's Five O'Clock Club. He'd just finished a performance and the manager asked him to stay for another week. It's reported that he told the manager that he was leaving the singing business, that he was going to become an actor. Harry's managers weren't really surprised. Belafonte had been doing well, making three or four hundred dollars a week. The women fans really liked him, but his managers knew that Belafonte didn't like what he was doing.

The Harry Belafonte that the public today is most familiar with wears an open-necked silk shirt, tight black pants and a big belt, but the one who sang in Miami wore a mustache, a tuxedo, a soulful expression and often sang while sitting on a high stool. He sang love songs to the ladies, with his hands folded in his lap.

Belafonte claims when he went backstage after singing his "pop ditties," he'd look at himself in the mirror and ask who he was kidding with the stuff.

In spite of the fact that Belafonte did not like what he was doing, that he quit, and that he wasn't really a big success as a pop singer, critics have noted that even then he had the mark of success of an up-and-coming singer. His sound had an identity, he just needed development and a different direction, one that would be interesting to him so that he could project more enthusiasm.

When Belafonte walked away from pop singing, he left good money and engagements that many singers would have been grateful to obtain. However, even though Harry may have been making $350 a week in Miami, most of the money went for agents, publicity, and Belafonte's mismanagement. Perhaps because he'd been poor as a child, any money he'd receive was often spent right away on expensive clothes and the like, according to friends of that period.

Harry has said that he was constantly in debt at that time, that he often thought that he couldn't keep going, that he'd have to get a regular job in order to take care of his family. Two factors probably influenced his decision to quit singing pop and jazz. One was the fact that he didn't believe in what he was doing; the other was that he was not providing a stable income for his wife and daughter.

The fact that he might make a good salary during one engagement was always countered by the fact that he might not work at all the next week. His wife was a teacher and used to a stable income. Perhaps if he'd been really doing well financially with his singing the family would have looked upon it with more favor. However, not only was he not providing well for them with his singing, but also his friends and his bohemian lifestyle were unacceptable to Margurite and her mother, who was living with them.

Margurite's mother had moved to New York in order to take care of baby Adrienne while her daughter continued teaching. There was not enough money to support the household unless Margurite continued to teach. It has been pointed out that while Belafonte really needed love and encouragement, he met with disapproval because of his profession and lack of formal education from his mother-in-law and his wife.

It is also noted that one of the things he loved about Julie, his second wife, was that her parents immediately accepted him. However, at the point when Julie's par-

Performer, Husband, Father

ents met Harry he was a successful, wealthy man, and in 1950 Belafonte was not really making it.

Belafonte's life was not good at home. Fortunately he had a group of friends who accepted him. With them he would eventually start a restaurant, and among them he would search for a singing style that would become folk singing.

Perhaps the fact that Harry decided to open The Sage indicates that he understood there was an imbalance between himself and Margurite in the employment area. It would seem that he was trying to be fair and helpful. Margurite had to leave her child at home while she went out and taught other people's children. She had been brought up to believe that it was the man's job to support the family.

When Harry and Margurite were first dating in New York, their heavy discussions centered around Harry's hostility to whites and the whole racial question. Now the topic of their disagreements became the question of what makes a home. They disagreed on what a man does with his dreams. Instead of heated discussions about discrimination against blacks, the subject became employment and commitment, especially when Harry was out of work.

Mrs. Byrd's presence in the Belafonte household, and her lack of acceptance of her son-in-law, did not help the domestic situation. Neither she nor her daughter liked Harry's friends, and the friends felt uncomfortable visiting Belafonte in his fourth floor walk up. It is reported that Harry never called her anything but Mrs. Byrd, until later when he started calling her nicknames given her by his children.

As mentioned above, not only did Mrs. Byrd disapprove of Harry's failure to earn money and his profession and friends, but she did not like the fact that he was uneducated. All of the children in her family had college degrees. It has been noted that in the Forties and Fifties there was fierce pride among many blacks who had educations. One of the reasons there was disapproval among the black community when Belafonte wanted to divorce Margurite nine years later, was because he was divorcing a black teacher.

His mother-in-law's rejection of him was of no encouragement or help to the struggling Belafonte. He was already very sensitive about his lack of education, one of the things that made him pretentious in his early years as a star.

Facing disapproval from his family, and having just given up pop singing, Harry decided to make some money while he decided what to do next in the professional arena. He opened a small restaurant with a friend in Greenwich Village. Even though The Sage did not succeed as a business venture, it was the place where Belafonte became Belafonte, the folk singer.

Chapter Three
The Folk Singer

In 1950 Belafonte and two friends opened The Sage restaurant in Greenwich Village. Although the restaurant was doomed to fail after eight months, this was the time and the nurturing place where Harry would find his career as a ballad and folk singer. It was here at The Sage where he sang with his friends. At home he was made to feel uncomfortable congregating with his "Bohemian" buddies. The Sage was a haven for Belafonte not only because he and his friends couldn't vocalize and carry on in Belafonte's home, but also because it was free from prejudice that often made Harry angry. When he'd had his engagement in Miami, Harry had been forced to obey a Negro curfew as well as other segregation ordinances. As will be seen in later chapters, the black entertainer in the Forties and Fifties had to endure humiliating racial prejudices and restrictions.

However, at The Sage there was nothing but friendship and fun. Bill Attaway, a black novelist, and Ferman Phillips, a developing black actor, opened the restaurant with Belafonte. The idea was to make enough money to eat and pay their bills, so that they would be able to be more selective about their careers.

Unchained by normal conventions and inhibitions in terms of lifestyles and sex, Greenwich Village was and is an area in New York City were young, creative people live an existence that is more conducive to the flowering of their talents and individuality than elsewhere. The Village is also where creative people wait for their talents to be recognized. The Sage was really a hamburger joint where Bill Attaway flipped the hamburgers in a front window while Harry waited tables and the counter. The story goes that the name "Sage" came about because the signmaker had those four letters left from another job, and so the penniless proprietors got them cheap.

The atmosphere was that of a Village greasy spoon—the place was patronized by poor Village residents, jazz musicians, theatre people, alcoholics, dopers, folk singers and hoods. The staff clowned around with the clientele. Tony Scott, the jazz clarinetist who later became Harry's musical arranger and conductor, spent time at The Sage, along with others who were to be a part of Belafonte' entourage when he became a star.

The real action at The Sage was after hours. When the place closed down to customers during the week, at two a.m., it became a rehearsal hall. Soloist and conductor of the male chorus was Harry. The rest of the chorus was made up of the unpaid waiters and friends. The fact that Belafonte became interested in folk singing in the Village is not unusual. Greenwich Village has always had a strong folk tradition. Because the Village is a mecca for artists and writers, and as a Bohemia that holds in high esteem freedom of expression and behavior, it has always emphasized values that are characteristically folk in type.

Not only did the Village foster Harry's growing interest in folk music, but so also did the characters who stopped in at The Sage. For example, one of the customers and members of the chorus was a Jewish cantor, Morty Freeman, who acquainted Harry with "Hava Nagilah" and other Israeli folk songs. Before long Belafonte was taking folk music very seriously. On weekends he traveled to Washington in order to dig through the archives of the Library of Congress for folk songs. He bought every folk record he could find. He became very interested in folklore.

Once he found songs of interest, he and his friends would spend two or three days working out arrangements. Bill Attaway, who later became Harry's collaborator on many folk adaptations and wrote scripts and record album liners for him, helped rewrite the words to songs Harry had found in the library or from some other source. Millard Thomas, a friend and a guitarist, who later became Harry's accompanist, wrote or changed the melody. Sometimes Millard's pupil, Craig Work, toiled with the melodies.

This time after hours at The Sage was invaluable, essential to Belafonte's formation as a singer. The Sage created a relaxed atmosphere with no audience to worry about. Harry had a chance to experiment and learn, to try out things for the first time. His fellow workers were able to notice the appeal of Harry's good looks to the women, when on occasion there were women present after hours.

The Sage was a place where Belafonte got in touch with himself as a singer of folk songs, and it was also the place where he met his second manager, Jack Rollins, who was to bring Harry close to the edge of stardom. It was not a place where Belafonte or any of the others met with financial success. As a matter of fact, Harry lost $2000 of his savings to the enterprise.

The three owners were not businessmen, nor did they have any working capital. Perhaps one of the reasons Belafonte had been so willing to go through with the restaurant idea, in spite of the fact that he had neither training nor financial backing, was to please his wife and show her he could earn a living in business. In reality, Margurite only visited the restaurant two or three times.

After eight months, Belafonte and Attaway sold the restaurant. It had not been a financial success, but it had been a laboratory for the future folk singer. It was an informal place where people would drop in and sit down. People could just sit and talk in the warm atmosphere. The food wasn't very good, but there was an air of excitement and hope at The Sage. It was a place where Belafonte could and did find himself. The people who frequented The Sage helped mold Belafonte. The nightly song fests and Harry's research trips to the Library of Congress helped him in his formation as a folk singer.

The Folk Singer

After The Sage closed, the group moved their rehearsals to the apartment of Tony Scott, the clarinetist. They also played baseball every Sunday. These days of Harry's association with Bill Attaway, Tony Scott, Millard Thomas and others was a combination of fun and hard work. It is said that even in those days, before Belafonte became famous, he was the center of attention among his friends. They depended upon him for laughs, for excitement, for strength. He was and has remained a man with a tremendous amount of energy.

Soon Tony met Fran, who was to become his wife, and they took a loft apartment on Fourth Avenue in the Village. It was here that The Sage gang continued their songs and their parties.

The experiments with folk music continued. Harry responded to folk music with an enthusiasm he'd never demonstrated toward jazz-pop music. He became more and more interested in folk music. The lack of sincerity Harry had protested in pop songs was not present in folk songs. He found them honest, pure of lyric and of beat. He could sing them with conviction and emotion.

There were other folk singers around in 1959; Burl Ives, Josh White and the Weavers sang folk ballads. However, Belafonte dramatized the old folk songs and gave them an intense emotional quality that was not present in the other singers' renditions of the ballads. Harry gave folk songs fire and passion. He felt that the nature of folk singing was dramatic. He decided not to play his own accompaniment on a guitar, as many folk singers did, because he wanted to be free to use his hands dramatically.

While originally Belafonte studied and explored folk

music to know his own people's traditions, to find a culture in which he could learn, he ended up finding a type of music in which he could function. He never felt he was contributing anything as a pop or jazz singer. As a folk singer he could use all his dramatic training and his voice to do something he really liked.

However, Belafonte still needed maturing and promoting before his folk songs were to make his fortune. While he was back at The Sage, a very important man came into his restaurant for a cup of coffee and stayed to become Harry's second manager and the person who got Belafonte's career off the ground.

Jack Rollins was an assistant to a threatrical producer, Max Gordon, at the time he met Belafonte. After getting to know Harry and becoming interested in pushing him as a ballad singer, he dropped all other obligations to manage Belafonte. From 1951 until Christmas of 1954 he molded, perfected and sold Belafonte to the public, bringing him to the edge of stardom. At the end of 1954, Harry rather unceremoniously fired him, having found a manager who he thought could do more for him. In spite of the fact that Belafonte's third manager, who he fired also, was able to get him bigger bookings than Rollins, it is generally agreed that it was Rollins who turned Belafonte into a magnificent folk singer.

Fortunately, Rollins' background was in the theater, and he was able to see the dramatic potential in Harry. Rollins first had to get Harry to find a style of his own. Belafonte was imitating the styles of other popular folk singers. He and Rollins began rehearsing every day.

Harry needed to learn diction, phrasing and how to make contact with the audience. Rollins worked to make Harry not only good but also commercial. Rollins

The Folk Singer

and Harry worked on the singer's clothes for his engagements. They worked on effective lighting, entrances, exits. Rollins and Harry worked and sweated so that Harry could ripen and mature as an artist and a performer.

It has been said that Rollins was devastated when he was suddenly fired by Belafonte. They had been like brothers, working together constantly. Rollins, having dropped everything in order to work with Harry, was left with nothing. He'd become too close, too involved, and Rollins became very bitter about the rupture.

However, during the years Rollins was working with Harry, he must have enjoyed seeing Belafonte becoming a success under his direction. The first place where Rollins booked the now more polished Belafonte was The Village Vanguard. This Greenwich Village club had introduced such entertainers as Zero Mostel, Josh White and Judy Holliday. When Rollins got the Vanguard engagement for Harry, the Scotts (Tony and Fran) and Bill Attaway sent out announcements. They helped fill the club, using the mailing lists of several black organizations, as well as sending cards to all The Sage customers.

Harry Belafonte was a sensation at the Vanguard. From this moment on he began to climb to the top, to become the first folk singer in history to command a mass audience. He stepped onto the stage in an outfit he and Rollins had assembled from clothing found in and representative of Greenwich Village. Instead of his tux and thin moustache, he was wearing an open-necked shirt and a wide belt. The audience, especially the women, went crazy.

He sang for twenty minutes to a spellbound audience,

and then he was called back for encores. The critics praised Belafonte. *Variety* found him impressive and commented favorably on his "feeling for the ancient folk tunes."

Belafonte had sung folk songs and calypso. Barry Ulanov, the jazz critic, wrote in *Metronome* in January of 1952 that: "Harry has the most attractive package in the folk music field. Combining his newly found stentorian tones with the unrestrained guitar of Craig Work, Harry moves and tears his way through a remarkable variety of songs—Negro and Brazilian Negro, American white and European—the best of the music that man has made and hasn't signed, the best of the music of the primitive and untutored." Ulanov felt that Harry's music moved many to tears, that, "it also makes much of a music that has been prettied and fussed and turned tastelessly indoors in the past. Here, it has a beat and a boom and a fine representative quality."

It seemed that not only was Belafonte an exciting performer who was to become a great success, but his protest over the Negro's position in the American culture was welcomed and heard.

Belafonte remained at the Vanguard for fourteen weeks. He was such a success that his manager was able to book him at an uptown nightclub, The Blue Angel. He overwhelmed the audience there. This time *Variety*, which had only praised him slightly when he appeared at the Village Vanguard, had nothing but approval. The trade paper said that Belafonte was the strongest point of the nightclub bill, that he'd progressed so much since his appearance in the Village that he could draw an uptown crowd. *Variety* wrote that his ballads had style,

The Folk Singer

class and feeling, and that with a widening catalog he would be able to assume concert stands.

Variety predicted concerts, and in a few years Belafonte was to give a concert at Lewisohn Stadium to the largest audience that had ever attended a show in that amphitheatre. At The Blue Angel, Harry was so popular that he was asked to remain for four months. His showmanship and his dramatic style, his American, Brazilian and calypso songs delighted the East Side people. He was accompanied by Millard Thomas.

After The Blue Angel, Rollins booked him into Philadelphia. Then, in June of 1952, he returned to the Vanguard. The critics said he was an innovator in the folk singing field with few peers.

Even though neither Harry nor Jack Rollins were making much money during this period, it was evident that Belafonte was on his way to the dizzying top. His friends of the time said he had charm, vitality and an ever-interested ranging mind; he read voraciously and in a variety of areas. He also had a restlessness about him that kept him always on the go. After his performance, Harry liked to party until early in the morning. His personality has been likened to Frank Sinatra, who is also charming, has a probing mind and is always moving. Belafonte was on his way, even though he didn't handle money well, and he really wasn't making that much on a regular basis. Both he and Rollins knew Harry needed to be pushed further.

The next things to be arranged for the up-and-coming performer were a major record contract and a part in a film. Also during this period Belafonte played the famous Thunderbird in Las Vegas, where he encountered some painful racial prejudice. Before 1952 was over, Harry had also appeared at a club in Queens, New York, and one in Hollywood. Although he was a rising star, not all of these engagements and contracts met with success.

The film in which Belafonte played was MGM's *The Bright Road*. Harry played the principal of a Southern school and Dorothy Dandridge played the role of a schoolteacher. The story, one to which Belafonte was sympathetic, was of a disturbed black schoolboy who was saved from becoming a delinquent by his sensitive schoolteacher. The teacher helped him find himself.

Unfortunately, not only was Belafonte's part not very big, but also, the film was not well-received. The criticism was that the film dealt too timidly with racial and economic questions. Although Belafonte sang a blues song, "Suzanne," which he wrote with Millard Thomas, he didn't receive much notice for his part in the film. If he'd been hoping that this would be his break, he was profoundly disappointed.

Belafonte's record contract with RCA Victor didn't bring much recognition or income either at this point. His first recordings were "A-Roving" and a folk ballad, "Chimney Smoke." These did not sell. His next record was "Man Smart," a calypso song, and "Jerry," a protest song. Finally, on his third try, "Scarlet Ribbons" and "Shenandoah," his records sold better. However, Belafonte was not really doing well in the record business.

As for his nightclub bookings, at the Thunderbird in Las Vegas he got very good reviews, even if he had to endure being treated as less than a man because he was

The Folk Singer

black. It has often been noted by black performers who worked in the Fifties, the years when blacks had to break down so many color barriers in the entertainment world, that they were always two people at once. If a performer was famous, he was applauded and paid well. But when he came off the stage, he was treated like a second-class citizen. In those days he still couldn't stay in the white man's hotel, eat in the hotel's restaurants or socialize in the hotel. No wonder so many black performers wound up on the psychiatrist's couch! It is thanks to performers like Belafonte, who refused to accept their segregation, that this was changed, at least for the most part.

However, in 1952, Belafonte wasn't ready to challenge the segregation in the Jim Crow town of Las Vegas. He wanted to rebel, but the booking was too important to him. Fortunately, a friend was able to give him some help, and Harry was a success at the Thunderbird.

The problem at the Thunderbird was that neither Harry nor his accompanist, Millard Thomas, were able to stay at the hotel where they were booked because they were black. Harry became angry and depressed when he and Millard were driven to a broken-down boarding house on the edge of town. He could neither sleep there nor could he feel like putting on a performance. For Belafonte's type of singing he had to be very enthusiastic, very self-confident. Also, Harry didn't have any money, so he couldn't think about moving to another place.

Their first rehearsal at the hotel was half-hearted. Fortunately Harry, feeling hurt, confused, resentful and unhappy, ran into a friend, Pete Kameron, a manager. Kameron got the manager of the Thunderbird to give Harry an advance, and he found Harry and Millard a better place to stay. The story goes that he told the motel manager that Harry and his friend were Latin.

Perhaps the best thing Kameron did for Belafonte was to give him some self-confidence. The room at the Thunderbird was big, and so was the stage.

He took the room by storm, according to *Variety*. He first sang a song about rebellion, "Jerry," and then the soft love song "Shenandoah." His Mississippi riverboat narrative, "Mark Twain," was next, followed by the calypso song, "Man, Smart-Woman Is Smarter." In the last-mentioned song he used his famous Jamaican accent. Then he sang the haunting "Scarlet Ribbons," and the Negro work song, "John Henry." His act ended with the calypso, "Hold 'Em Joe." He was written up as "highly kinetic" and as a singer whose sense of the dramatic in his songs made him magical.

Although Belafonte's engagement was successful, the racial prejudice made him unhappy. He couldn't use the casino, the dining rooms, the cocktail lounges or the pool. He could only visit with friends if they came backstage. In 1955 Belafonte was to again play Vegas, this time as a star. He would at this time break down many of the color barriers, so that he and other black performers would no longer be humiliated.

After Las Vegas, Harry returned to New York to do an engagement in November at a huge dance hall on Queens Boulevard. Playing to a young, rowdier group, Harry was a success. He hypnotized the crowd with his presence. *Billboard* reviewer Bill Smith wrote:

The Folk Singer

"Belafonte has seldom worked better, appeared to better advantage or worked to a more enthusiastic audience than he has here at The Boulevard. From a poor start as a bop singer some years ago, the tall slim Belafonte is rapidly becoming the top folk singer in the business. As he went into familiar items now on RCA Victor, the huge mob rocked with him with such zest that it took on an almost hysterical frenzy more often associated with a Johnny Ray audience . . ."

Belafonte was not much of a success at The Ambassador in Hollywood. Still, his appearance at the Ambassador's world famous Coconut Grove did constitute a breakthrough; Harry was the first black to play there. Perhaps because he had not been well-publicized on the West Coast, Harry did not draw big crowds at the Coconut Grove. Later, Harry would pack them in at Hollywood's Greek Theater. In a few years he would be taking Hollywood and all of Europe by storm.

By the end of 1952 Harry's friends considered him a success. He'd been accepted in New York City, and he'd been in a Hollywood film. They threw a party for him. Harry's wife, Margurite, was there for a while, but the cavorting around was not comfortable for her, so she left early. Marlon Brando was there, as well as Belafonte's other friends. Their buddy Harry was doing very well.

Chapter Four
The Ascending Star

Belafonte's career was taking off, but at a moderate pace. The beginning of 1953 saw him being booked and accepted at better and better night spots. By the middle of 1953 he was getting serious analytical attention from the trade publications. Then, in 1954, his ascent to the top became quicker. Belafonte starred in his first movie, acted in major roles in two theatrical productions of worth and continued to be a success in nightclubs. Belafonte at this time became a father for the second time, met the woman who was to be his second wife, and broke with his dedicated manager Jack Rollins. After 1954, Harry's career and life would move at a breakneck pace.

Early in 1953 Harry was asked to record a Japanese folk-type song, "Gomen-Nasai." Although Belafonte did not feel this song was his style, he recorded it. This was the first of Belafonte's songs to sell, even though it was not a smash. At least the recording sales pleased RCA Victor enough that they renewed his contract. Belafonte never sang the Japanese song in his club dates. He was a perfectionist who had very good taste and knew what songs were good for him. He also did an excellent job of choosing his arrangers and arrangements, as well as his musicians. One of the people associated with Harry's recording days in the early Fifties also comments that Belafonte was articulate to the point of being pedantic, especially when it came to ethnic issues.

His big night club success in 1953 was at The Black Orchid in Chicago. Not only was he praised as a performer in his own right, but he was compared favorably with Josh White, who had the singing engagement before Belafonte. When Harry had played at The Blue Angel, a critic had written that Belafonte had a long way to go to assume the authority of Josh White.

Now, in Chicago, the critics praised Belafonte's performance, calling him "electrifying." He filled the room for his performances in spite of the fact that he was less well known than Josh White. The difference between Belafonte and White and other folk singers was that Belafonte did not play a guitar. Instead, he used his hands, face and body to dramatize his songs.

Harry was an actor on the stage. He created a theater of the folk ballad. He expressed strong emotions, overwhelmed the audience and even got them to participate. Belafonte is known for songs in which he has the audience sing responses and choruses. Thus the image of the relaxed folk singer with his guitar was changed by the dynamic Belafonte.

Although Belafonte could well be proud of his reception at The Black Orchid, he was lonely being away from home. It has been said that this is a major drawback of being an entertainer, having to travel and be alone so much. If Harry were more successful in 1953, perhaps he would have been less lonely. However, he was still far from being a superstar, so the time alone was filled with uncertainty.

Also, in view of the fact that Belafonte had not had a real home life as a child, being on the road tended to make him insecure. He often had friends staying with him. Sometimes he called his wife Margurite and had her come stay with him. Also there was the temptation of the women who make advances at handsome entertainers on the road. There were gossip column items about Harry and various women. His wife tried to ignore the gossip columnists. However, her husband's being on the road so much did nothing to keep the couple close. Margurite still did not like Harry's profession.

After RCA Victor renewed Belafonte's contract, he recorded "Matilda, Matilda," one of his most successful songs. Actually, the successful version was a re-recording done in 1955. It was that one that appeared in his famous *Calypso* album.

The 1955 recording was done in Hollywood with an instrumental group that approximated a band of the swing era, and it was arranged by Tony Scott. The first recording was done in New York with three fiddles, three clarinets, three drummers and a seven-piece vocal group. Even before Belafonte became a star he was a perfectionist. Even though the money for recording comes out of the artist's royalties, Belafonte would not let go of a song until it was done as well as he could make it.

To anyone who has heard Belafonte in concert, it is this song, "Matilda, Matilda," that gets the audience going. It's the one where Belafonte makes the audience join in on the choruses, "ladies over forty," and "big spenders, be still." "Now the intellectuals!" Thus, in retrospect, it's possible to see that Belafonte was on his way in 1953, because he was recording one of his hit songs. However, the song did not become a hit until it was released several years later in the *Calypso* album.

Even though his recordings weren't big hits yet, Harry was, in 1953, starting to attract attention in the trade newspapers. *Down Beat* wrote about him more than once during 1953. In one article a critic described Belafonte as having universality, of appealing to all kinds of audiences and to their emotions. When Harry was singing, the differences between people just melted away. Not only could he sing calypso numbers with electricity, but he did a fantastic rendition on stage of the old "Scarlet Ribbons," and his version of the Israeli song "Hava Nagilah" was spectacular.

An article in *Down Beat* in November of 1953 reviewed Belafonte's re-appearance at The Boulevard in Queens. This was the nightspot where the raucous audience was so hard for performers to capture. But, just as with the first time Belafonte had spellbound the group; he again mesmerized them. The critic Nat Hentoff wrote that Belafonte had achieved an unprecedented power and prestige as a folk singing act. The article pointed out that Harry was successful in some of the country's top night clubs, where others had not succeeded.

It seemed Belafonte had the ability to command the attention of an audience, even difficult groups. In the Queens nightclub there were always problems of people talking during shows. Still, when Belafonte started out with his dynamic song "Timber," the audience became still. He stood, handsome in his open necked shirt and accompanied by his guitarist, Millard Thomas and charmed the group. One song, "Hold 'Em Joe," enraptured the audience with the tale of an Alabama preacher chanting a sermon at the death of Lincoln.

At the Queens nightclub, as with his other appearances, he was called back for encores.

As the year 1953 came to a close, it was evident that Belafonte was on his way. *Billboard* chose him for its "Talent Showcase of 1954," a real honor to a newcomer. He was also signed to appear in a Broadway show produced by John Murray Anderson.

Perhaps Belafonte felt he was becoming successful, for he decided to buy a two-story house in Elmhurst, Long Island. His daughter, Adrienne, was four, and it was time for his family to move from 156th Street and Amsterdam Avenue in the city.

He was not a star yet, so he couldn't afford his dream-house. This is why they settled for a duplex with small rooms. Still, it was much better than raising a child on the traffic-filled streets of New York City. The neighborhood was white, so when the Belafonte's moved in, "for sale" signs started appearing. Later, the neighborhood became integrated, with blacks on one side of the street and the whites on the other side.

The John Murray Anderson production, named *Almanac*, opened on Broadway on December 10, 1953. This was the first of Belafonte's important performances. In 1954 he would also star in a film, as well as appear in a second major theatrical production.

Although Belafonte received awards and praise for his role in *Almanac*, he actually was not in an acting role in the play. He sang three songs in the production—"Hold 'Em Joe," "Acorn in the Meadow," and "Mark Twain," which he had written. When it was time to accept one of the awards, it is said that he became suddenly ill and had to send his wife to receive the award for him.

However, whether or not Belafonte considered himself unsuccessful because he only sang in the play, his performance netted him a starring role in a Hollywood movie and an acting role in another theatrical production.

Almanac opened at the Imperial Theater in 1953. Although the play contained successful people, and the music was written by Adler and Ross, who later did the scores for *Pajama Game* and *Damn Yankees*, the play was not a success. In some of the notices, Belafonte wasn't mentioned. However, in the ones where he was mentioned he received nothing but praise. The *New York Times* said he was electrifying and stunning. Another paper wrote that, although he wasn't on stage for long, he was outstanding.

For this role, Belafonte received the Antoinette Perry or "Tony" award as "the best supporting actor of the

The Ascending Star

year," and the *Billboard* Donaldson Award "for the best supporting actor in a musical show." Although the Tony and the Donaldson were sought after by actors, Belafonte was receiving dramatic awards for being a folk singer. He probably felt this was not bringing him closer to his goal, which was still to be an actor. It was almost as if he was becoming a successful, soon to be world-famous singer, in spite of himself.

During his run in *Almanac*, Belafonte was also appearing at a club on East 54th Street, and recording for RCA Victor at approximately the same time. The club, La Vie En Rose, paid him a high salary, although the figures differ from source to source. His show was so good in this swanky club that one critic wrote he had run out of superlatives to describe Belafonte's work.

His recording sessions went on, but at this point did not produce a hit record. Thus, even though he was a hit in *Almanac* and a great success at La Vie En Rose, he was not a hit in the record business. RCA Victor released "Acorn in the Meadow" and "Hold 'Em Joe," both from *Almanac*, but they did not sell.

An album was recorded around "Mark Twain," called *Mark Twain and Other Favorites*. Although there was some calypso-type music in the album, it consisted mainly of English, American and Scottish folk ballads. The album did not sell well. Not until 1955 did it finally start to move. However, by 1957 the *Calypso* album became a runaway hit, then *Mark Twain and Other Favorites* became a fast seller, as well as almost everything that Belafonte had recorded before.

Mark Twain contained new versions of old folk songs, such as the old English sea chantey, "The

Drummer and the Cook," and "Tol' My Captain," an American chain gang song. These versions were by Pete Kameron (using another name), the man who had been so helpful to Belafonte with the racial discrimination in Las Vegas.

Even though Harry was feeling frustrated as an actor, despite his spiraling success as a singer, it was his singing that got him his role in the film *Carmen Jones*. While Belafonte was quoted in *Newsweek* at this time as saying his singing was like "having big brother overshadow you all the time." Otto Preminger was making his mind up to star Harry in the film.

Preminger, the Hollywood producer, was casting for Oscar Hammerstein II's modernized, all-black version of the Bizet opera, *Carmen*. When he saw Belafonte in *Almanac*, he knew he had found his male lead. On April 29, 1954, Belafonte was signed to play the role of Joe, the soldier who tragically falls in love with Carmen, the cigarette girl.

In May, Belafonte arrived in Hollywood for the third time. Two years earlier he had filmed *The Bright Road* for MGM in Hollywood, and the year before he'd been the first black to play the swanky Coconut Grove in the Hotel Ambassador.

Carmen Jones had been a hit as a Broadway operatic musical, and it was a box-office success as a movie. Still, the movie critics did not consider it a great movie. Belafonte received mixed reviews. One critic wrote that he was static and not very heroic in his role; that he was "lost in a vortex of confusion rather than a nightmare of shame." However, other critics admired Harry's acting, especially the torrid love scenes. There was one

The Ascending Star

scene in which Harry kissed Carmen's big toe that was signaled out as passionate.

This production of *Carmen* concentrated a great deal of its attention on the spoken word and the drama, rather than on singing. In *Carmen Jones* there was as much dialogue as there was song. Harry was able to use his acting talents more than he did in *Almanac*. One critic wrote that Dorothy Dandridge and Harry Belafonte were wonderful to look at, and that they really delivered in the film.

The Bizet opera in the film *Carmen Jones* is set in a parachute factory in the South and in a prize-fight stadium in Chicago. Carmen meets Joe (Harry), who is a soldier, in a parachute factory. She wins him away from his childhood love, Cindy Lou. She finally causes him to desert the Army and flee to Chicago. Since Carmen is forced to remain in hiding with Joe, she finally grows restless and takes up with a prize fighter. Then Joe demands that she come back to him, but she refuses. In a final climactic scene he strangles her to death.

This role was very important to Belafonte. For the first time, he had a dramatic role in a major film or dramatic production. This had been a dream of his since the all-important night in 1946 when he'd seen his first play in the American Negro Theater. Although Harry did not sing in *Carmen Jones*—the music being dubbed in by Levern Hutcherson, who sang Porgy in Broadway's *Porgy and Bess*—he took his acting extremely seriously. Harry's zest for work made him give his all to the performance. Dorothy Dandridge, who played Carmen in this film, was to star with Harry in other film productions.

If *Carmen Jones* was important to Belafonte because it gave him his first opportunity to be a film star, it was also important historically to Harry. Belafonte has during his career as a singer and actor done much to better the lot of the black performer. *Carmen Jones* was the first all-black film to become a box-office success. It was important to Belafonte that pictures with black artists, dealing with the folklore of Negro life, be commercially successful.

Belafonte made his second appearance at the Coconut Grove while in Hollywood. This time, in August, 1954, his engagement was commercially successful. *Variety* wrote that the "opening night crowd was pounding for more." He sang a beautiful gospel shout, "Noah," in which he was only accompanied by drums.

Harry was to return to the East Coast in time for the birth of his second daughter, Shari. He was also to become involved in a second theatrical production before the year was out. However, while still on the West Coast, another major thing happened to Belafonte besides his Hollywood film and his success at the Coconut Grove—he met his second wife-to-be, Julie Robinson.

When Harry met Julie in 1954, his marriage with Margurite was not going well. He had often spent the night with his friends Tony and Fran Scott, while playing in *Almanac*, rather than return home to Elmhurst. The problem was what in a court of law is called "incompatibility." Margurite had a certain concept of home and family. To her, being a working mother and having a husband who was away a lot was not a proper family. Harry, on the other hand, was committed to his show business way of life, which to Margurite was anathema.

This stalemate made Belafonte very unhappy, for he did not want his marriage to fall apart. However, Harry was a man who needed companionship and acceptance. His loneliness as a child without a father made his need for affection greater than perhaps someone else's would be. He could not get companionship from a woman who disapproved of his friends, his outlook on life, his ambitions. Harry and his wife did not share the same interests. By 1954 it appeared that feeling was gone from their marriage. The situation was made even more difficult by the expectation of the new baby. So many couples think that having a baby will make their marriage close again, only to find out that it often worsens the relationship. Perhaps Margurite did not realize how far apart she and Harry had drifted.

Because he was not getting what he needed at home, Belafonte turned to friends in New York and on the road. He was ripe for a woman who could give him companionship when he met Julie while filming *Carmen Jones*.

Julie Robinson, white, Jewish and a dancer, had lived a very interesting life before she met Belafonte. Born in New York City, she was the second daughter of Clara and George Robinson. Since her sister was ten years older than she, and her parents were middle-aged when she was born, Julie, like Harry, was a rather lonely child. While quite young she demonstrated two aspects of her character that were to be important to her. Perhaps these traits came out of her loneliness. One was her artistic flair; the other was her identification with minorities, and in general, humanitarianism.

The artistic impulse, after attending the Little Red School House in Greenwich Village, took her to the

High School of Music and Art. She had a good ear for music, and an ability for drawing. Nevertheless, it was dancing that became her passion. The humanitarian drive was first manifested as a love for animals, later as friendship and sympathy for outcasts. She later became quite active on behalf of the NAACP. Something in her loneliness responded to the rejection and discrimination suffered by blacks in society. Many of her playmates were black, since she did not feel identity with her own culture. Belafonte felt left out from his culture, being too dark for his relatives' approval. His childhood had been filled with some of the same feelings that Julie had felt.

Julie Robinson was also an impulsive, carefree bohemian from her early years on. She grew up developing an interest in other cultures besides her own. Languages were easy for her to learn, and she traveled, having an easy ability to enter into other people's way of life.
life.

She became determined to become a dancer, and it was the Katherine Dunham Company to which she wanted to belong. The Dunham Company was an all-black dance company and one of the leading dance groups in the Forties. Although Julie was small and dark, with long braids, she was not black. Finally, after demonstrating tenacity, she was admitted to the company.

Being a fine dancer, a hard worker and a very dedicated person, she ultimately became a teacher in the group. Traveling with the group as their only white dancer, she insisted on standing by the other dancers when they encountered the racial prejudice that black

The Ascending Star

entertainers met in the Forties. Ertha Kitt, a fellow-dancer in the Dunham Company, shared a room with Julie in London when they performed in England for six months.

Julie's fellow dancers soon came to accept her, as she demonstrated true empathy for their problems and concerns. She has been described as animated, at ease with people, full of life and very excited about living.

Her travels with the dance company took her all over the world. By 1950 she was appearing as a featured dancer with the company. Her repertory included South American, Brazilian, tango, jazz and other forms of dance. After working with the company for about six years, she won their respect for identifying with their problems.

When Harry met her, Julie's father had gone into semi-retirement in Los Angeles and Julie was involved in some motion picture work. Known to be one of the girls Marlon Brando was seeing, it may have been Brando himself who took her onto the set of *Carmen Jones*.

She and Harry got along from the beginning. Just as Margurite had recommended books to Belafonte about Negro culture when they first met, so did Julie. She talked with him about the struggle of blacks against second-class citizenship and about the problems in Africa. They also could talk about jazz and folk music as well as other subjects.

Julie lent Harry some books. When he dropped by her house to pick up the volumes, he was pleased and surprised by her parents' reception. They were cordial and accepting. Also, their home was lively and warm, something he'd never known as a child. When it was time for Belafonte to return to New York, his life was a little different because of his meeting with Julie.

In New York in September of 1954, Harry's second child, Shari Lynn Belafonte, was born. Tony Scott was the godfather at her baptism into the Catholic Church. Shortly after returning home from the hospital, Margurite found out about Julie, or at least that a Julie Robinson was writing letters to her husband. Not having kept up with Harry's friends, she did not know who Julie was. Confronting her husband, it was perhaps then that she realized their marriage was crumbling. She warned him that scandal could wreck his career, which was on the verge of taking off. At this time he did not have answers for a lot of things, one of which was the direction in which his marriage was going.

It has been said by critics and writers that Harry needed a mother-type person in the beginning, because it gave him the strength and solidity of purpose he so much lacked because of his background. Perhaps by 1954, having become someone in his own right, he needed more companionship and acceptance than mothering. For whatever the reasons, Belafonte's marriage soon began to crumble. Perhaps at this stage his wife couldn't see the splitting; while Harry had been away from New York he had phoned her and Adrienne regularly. At home he was affectionate and considerate, if distracted. The marriage did not break up at this point, but the cracks were beginning to show.

Before the end of 1954 there was another theater production in the works. Belafonte planned to do a Negro folk musical; however, what he ended up doing was the unusual production, *Three For Tonight*, with Marge and Gower Champion.

"An Evening of Negro Folklore with Music," an idea that Belafonte worked on with producer Paul Gregory and actor Charles Laughton, who was to direct, never came about. In an interview with *Downbeat* before he left on tour with *Three for Tonight*, Belafonte described the project, which was by then called, "The Negro Anthology." Set to begin as a traveling show some time in 1955, it would have a company of fifty and would contain readings from black authors.

Said Belafonte: "It'll be as authentic as I can find and interpret it. We plan to go into and visit the chain gangs and prison camps in the South. I hope that by the time I'm forty that I'll be sufficiently established so that I can perform material that's even closer to the ethnic base than I do now."

In planning to do an ethnic and authentic black theater production, Belafonte was demonstrating an involvement with the advancing of black culture and economic success.

Nevertheless, in spite of Gregory's and Belafonte's initial plans to do a black folk play or anthology, Harry was instead starred by Paul Gregory in *Three For Tonight*. He left with Marge and Gower Champion on a fifteen-week tour of one-nighters. With the close of 1954, the beginning of his second major theatrical production and the completion of his first starring role in a motion picture, Belafonte was definitely on his way to stardom.

Chapter Five
Bittersweet Success

The years 1954 and 1955 were extremely successful ones for Belafonte. *Variety* reported at the end of 1955 that Harry Belafonte had earned $350,000 that year. He not only had a Broadway hit in 1955, but played in the country's most elegant clubs. Also in 1955, Belafonte appeared on TV, a medium that was not then too receptive to blacks. Belafonte was also able to help blacks as he crossed many color lines and did away with at least some racial restrictions while he toured with his play, and also in the nightclub area.

However, those years, if they brought great success to the performer, also brought traumas. Belafonte began seeing a psychiatrist, he changed managers and ultimately got rid of a third manager; his marriage worsened. Although he came out victorious in most cases,

BELAFONTE

Belafonte was forced to endure pain because of his blackness. It has been said that black entertainers have done much to help blacks by removing color barriers. However, the black entertainers were the ones who had to endure the pain of this discrimination in order to change it. For Harry, as with other blacks, he had to feel the anxiety of being famous and playing in posh nightclubs, while at the same time being discriminated against because he was black. There were many times when he was denied entrance to a club where he was playing by an uninformed waiter or other employee, because the waiter saw that he was black. Success brings trauma to anyone, but being black and a sudden success can really bring on stress.

Perhaps the most outstanding effect of Belafonte's success was his new stature in American society. Like others of his race, he'd been refused admittance to clubs, restaurants and hotels. Not only did this happen to him while on the road, but also in New York City. Now, because he was a success, he was asked to perform in some of those same places that had ostracized him before. Being at first excluded because he was black and then suddenly paid large sums of money to perform at the same places was disorienting to Harry.

Emotionally, the contrast between acceptance and rejection was hard enough to take, but there was more. Perhaps, as in Las Vegas, Harry would be applauded while he was on stage, but he would be just a black man once he stepped off stage, unable to use the hotel's facilities or stay in one of its suites. Thus there was that upsetting duality of being at one moment accepted and applauded only to be rejected at the next moment.

Success to a man who has come from poverty or from an underprivileged life must be shocking to the emotional system of one who achieves that kind of glory. There are many performers, Freddy Prinze, Elvis Presley, Janice Joplin and numerous others, whose deaths are testimony to the fact that success frequently exacts a terrible price. And the double-standard for black performers that prevailed at that time in Belafonte's life took its toll upon his sense of self-worth.

Then, there is the loss of privacy that comes with success. The star is constantly stared at, newspaper columnists write about his every move, and other performers watch him. This invasion of a star's privacy has caused breakdowns in more than one performer. Belafonte, feeling these pressures as his career became more and more successful, finally sought the help of a psychiatrist, Dr. Janet Alterman Kennedy.

Dr. Kennedy was a white analyst, a professor at Columbia University interested in the psychotherapy of black patients. In 1954 it is said that Belafonte saw her several times a week. The success that had been so crucial to him had become too much of a burden to bear alone, so he asked for help. Dr. Kennedy's husband, J. Richard Kennedy, was a stockbroker, sometime agent and author. He would become Belafonte's next manager, replacing Jack Rollins in 1954.

In 1953, it was Jack Rollins who introduced Harry to the Kennedys. There was a Festival of the Arts at the Tarleton Club. Belafonte was invited to do a program of folk songs, and Kennedy was there to discuss his new novel, *Prince Bart*. Playing the Tarleton Club in one of a series of one-night stands in the White Mountains of

New Hampshire set up for him by his manager Jack Rollins, Belafonte met the man who was to replace Rollins.

Rollins later charged that the Kennedys, through Dr. Kennedy's psychoanalysis, had persuaded Belafonte that he needed to change managers in order to better his business affairs. It is true that Kennedy, a more aggressive man than Rollins, was able to get bookings in some of the major clubs where Rollins had not been able to book Harry.

What actually happened was that Belafonte started his therapy, and eventually asked Kennedy to manage him. Rollins was still under contract as Belafonte's manager. The story goes that Kennedy called Rollins into his office one day and read him a letter. The letter stated that Belafonte did not wish to renew Rollins' contract.

There had been hints that Harry needed a manager to handle big deals, as his career was now getting more involved. But Rollins had felt like a brother to Belafonte, and his dismissal in this way hurt him. Had Belafonte gotten a manager to handle big deals, Rollins assumed he would still handle the artistic side of Harry's work.

Rollins felt he had been shafted both financially and morally. He filed a financial suit against Belafonte and an alienation suit against the Kennedys. Neither suit seems to have come to trial, and it's felt that there was an out-of-court agreement made.

Harry's treatment of Rollins has been questioned. Jack Rollins gave up all of his other work in order to devote himself to Harry's career. He helped Belafonte's career get off the ground, got him the contract with

Bittersweet Success

RCA Victor, his first date in Las Vegas, and his first movie contract. However, on the other side there is the fact that Belafonte may have felt he needed someone more aggressive as his career began to take off. Perhaps he had outgrown Rollins. It is said that Kennedy, a pushy, assertive man, acted as a father figure to the performer, taking care of his money and pushing him farther on. Kennedy got Belafonte into places that had not previously booked black performers—the Palmer House in Chicago and the Eden Roc in Miami, among others.

When people achieve success, they can change in certain ways. Not only did Belafonte get rid of Rollins, but he also fired Kennedy before his contract was up. Also, his marriage became worse under the pressures of success.

If life wasn't already complicated enough for Belafonte, his fifteen-week tour with the musical, *Three For Tonight*, would take him into some of the ultra-segregated areas of the South, involving him in many unsavory incidents.

The tour started in 1955, while the South was steaming over the Supreme Court decision to desegregate the schools. Belafonte had seen prejudice in his mixed neighborhood in Harlem and even in Elmhurst, Long Island, where his buying a house had made white neighbors move away. However, an extended tour in the South with a mixed company was a shocking revelation. Harry knew the possible problems, humiliations and even perils awaiting him by touring with a racially mixed company. It was important to him that he make the tour and its 94 one-night stands, even though it would take the *Three For Tonight* company into the "Jim Crow" South. Belafonte was interested in bringing about respect for his people. He, as well as other black entertainers, wanted to face the existing conditions in order to bring about an acceptance of the black performer in a mixed company by white Southern audiences.

There were many times on the tour when the cast had to perform in school auditoriums and gymnasiums because there were no theaters in the town. There were threats and events that were humiliating and unpleasant. Undaunted, the group kept trudging. Harry had to use Negro bathrooms and Negro water fountains and sleep in hotels for blacks only. He even had to sit in segregated sections of the airport.

There are numerous stories about the prejudice encountered during this tour. Harry and Millard Thomas, who was also black, had to sneak into hotels with the white members of the group. One story goes that a state trooper in Virginia entered the white men's room to find Belafonte and order him out. There is another happening recalled about Harry waiting in a Houston airport all night. It seems that Belafonte was usually housed with black leaders while traveling in the South. This time, because the group changed plans at the last minute and was scheduled to fly out of Houston in the morning, Belafonte was unable to find accommodations. He ended up spending the night in the airport.

The next day, after asking the ticket agent what time his plane was expected to arrive, it's reported that the agent, seeing a young, handsome black standing before him, replied that the plane would arrive when it was good and ready. A staring match ensued between the two. Luckily, a group of white high-school students came through the terminal and recognized Belafonte. As they were asking for autographs, the agent realized his mistake and found Belafonte's ticket.

This was typical of the confusion generated by Harry's acceptance as a performer and rejection as a human being. The more wealthy the performer became, the more confusing the situation became. There was constant admiration while on stage, followed by humiliation and rejection of Belafonte the human being. It was difficult for Belafonte as it has been difficult for other black performers to travel with shows. There are stories about black performers who actually had to perform when they were hungry because they couldn't locate a restaurant that would serve them.

There were, of course, many good moments on the tour, where Belafonte felt admiration and acceptance by Southern people. He was also able to meet some of the black leaders, those who tirelessly took cases to court and worked to get equality for their people. There was also prejudice toward blacks in other areas besides the South. There is a story about Harry's humiliation in Chicago in the same year, 1955, when he played the Palmer House. It's told how a maitre d' didn't recognize Belafonte, who was waiting in the wings for the preceding act to finish so he could make his entrance on stage. The maitre d' ordered him to leave the area.

Harry, angry and humiliated, left the stage and sat in the lobby. When it was time for his entrance, he was not to be found. Finally somebody spotted the famous folk singer and persuaded him to do his show. Later the maitre d' apologized, but the damage was done.

With the tour finally over, *Three For Tonight* opened on Broadway. The producer, Paul Gregory, had conceived of using Belafonte in a theater production after seeing him in *Almanac*. He was thrilled by Harry's folk singing and determined to do a musical of Negro folklore with him. After talking about the various types of plays, Gregory finally decided to use Belafonte in *Three For Tonight*, with Marge and Gower Champion.

The play, an off-beat musical, was done before drapes, with some stools and a music stand for props. Harry was a great success. In the musical he sang fourteen songs from his folk repertoire. For his role critics praised Belafonte, calling him brilliant, an artist of great consequence, a superlative performer. Brooks Atkinson of The *New York Times* wrote that Belafonte was magnificent, vibrant and magnetic, "all artist and a rousing performer. . . ."

There were also those reviewers who found fault with Belafonte's performance. One ongoing criticism by some was about Harry's pretentiousness. One critic suggested that Belafonte was too dramatic, another that his delivery was pretentious. There may have been some justification for this kind of criticism. Sometimes when performers become successful, without realizing it they lose some of their original simplicity. Or perhaps they become a bit smug or slick or mannered. Pretentiousness is a criticism often leveled at Belafonte in his dealings with people, too. However, for the most part, the reviews of *Three For Tonight* gave great praise to the performer.

1955 was also a year of night club accomplishments for Belafonte. He appeared as a headliner at the Copa in

New York. To a black entertainer in 1955, an engagement at the Copa meant a great deal. For one thing, to play at the Copa in 1955 was to have made it as a performer. Sammy Davis, Jr. and Frank Sinatra were the kinds of people who were asked to play the Copa.

Perhaps another reason why Belafonte would relish an engagement at the Copa would be the fact that years earlier he was not allowed entrance to the club when he tried to get in as a sailor. Even though he wore a uniform, because he was black he was denied entrance, at least that seems to have been the probable reason. To be the main attraction at the Copa must have been sweet vengeance for Belafonte.

Although the Copa was a difficult club to play because it was a supper club, where people ate, drank and talked, Belafonte was a howling success. He was able to spellbind his audiences with his combination of soft, gentle ballads and lively folk songs.

In order to keep his act from growing stylized, and also so that he could better adapt to the larger clubs, Harry and Tony Scott rearranged some of his work. Instead of just being accompanied by a guitar, in 1955 Harry started using an orchestra and/or chorus. He was an avid reader of his reviews and had a sharp, examining mind; thus he was very anxious that his work would keep growing and changing.

A jazz feeling was added to many of the folk numbers through the accompaniments, giving the folk music a distinctive beat. The *Calypso* album contains songs accompanied by the jazz texture. At the Copa Belafonte appeared with brass instruments, rather than just a guitar.

His new manager, Jay Richard Kennedy, had spurred Belafonte on to adding the instruments to his show. Kennedy at this time also got major bookings for his client. Harry played the Fairmont in San Francisco in August of 1955. Later he played the Waldorf in New York. Tony Scott, Harry's musical conductor, added black musicians to the Waldorf's regular white band for the performance. Belafonte was very well received at all of these bookings.

At the end of the year Belafonte opened the fashionable Cafe Pompeii at the Eden Roc in Miami. At this time Belafonte was to break through Miami's color barrier and thus be of help to his race. Five years earlier, while he had played at the Five O'Clock Club, he'd had to stay in a segregated hotel, use segregated transportation, use segregated restaurants, drinking fountains and toilets. This was the club where he'd done his last singing as a pop/jazz singer, where he'd walked out on his engagement.

When Harry had played the Five O'Clock Club blacks had to be off the street by nine p.m., unless they had written permission from an employer.

In 1955, when Belafonte played the Eden Roc, he was allowed to use all the facilities, thus being the first black in Miami's history to use the "white" hotel's facilities. Although he had endured humiliation as a black in some of the Southern towns while on tour with *Three For Tonight*, he was to finish the same year having integrated the white beaches of Miami.

1955 was also the year in which Belafonte appeared on television for the first time. Belafonte made two TV appearances in which he sang. He also appeared in a drama on the General Electric Theater. The play, *Winner By Decision*, was written by his friend Bill Attaway. Harry played the part of a prize fighter, with Ethel Waters playing his mother. Belafonte also did a TV version of *Three For Tonight*, for which he received critical praise.

So, 1955 was a successful year for Belafonte. It is reported that in 1955 he signed a deal with the Waldorf providing for two bookings annually at the highest salary ever paid a performer by that hotel.

Chapter Six
Crucial Times

In 1956, Belafonte was just around the corner from world-wide fame. The *Calypso* album would become a million dollar best seller in 1957. Not surprisingly, the times were strewn with chaos as well as stardom for Belafonte. Harry's nine-year marriage was to soon break up, and he was to threaten his relationship with his own people by marrying a white woman. 1956 brought a theatrical flop into Belafonte's shining career, and it also brought a break with his third manager, Jay Richard Kennedy. One of Belafonte's responses to stress, laryngitis, flared up and required surgery. And finally, during this chaotic period there were such triumphs as the concert at Lewisohn Stadium.

There are conflicting opinions about whether Belafonte asked Kennedy to manage him or whether Kennedy came into Harry's life through his wife, Belafonte's psychiatrist. There were also differences of opinion over just how helpful Kennedy was to Belafonte. Certainly, Kennedy was partly to blame for the flop, *Sing Man Sing*; he wrote the book, the lyrics and, with Belafonte, wrote the score.

Kennedy, a small man with a big style, was said to be an almost hypnotic talker, a very persuasive man. He was also said by some to be extremely emotional. One story tells of Kennedy being moved to tears by Harry's accounts of his humiliation because of color, his upbringing in a mixed neighborhood, rejection by his own relatives and indignities suffered later in life.

Kennedy was originally hired as a financial manager and adviser. Not only was he given power of attorney in order to make business deals for Belafonte, but he also became involved in Harry's songs and theater productions.

Belafonte's career really did soar under Kennedy's management. Kennedy, a millionaire several times in his life, had the aggressiveness and drive necessary to push Belafonte into bigger deals than Rollins was able to do. *Ebony* magazine wrote in March, 1956: "Millionaire Steers Folk Singer to Fame." The article, describing Kennedy as one of America's most remarkable businessmen, a millionaire financier and a talented writer and composer, wrote that, "When they joined forces, Belafonte shot close to the top of the entertainment world."

In the same article Kennedy was quoted as saying that all Harry needed was a few breaks. Harry was quoted as saying that Kennedy was a genius. However, within six months of the article's publication, Belafonte discharged Kennedy and became involved in more lawsuits. Kennedy's contract did not run out for almost two years.

The facts are jumbled. How can someone be wonderful, and then six months later be fired? In show business this is often the case. There is so much pressure, so much ego involved. Belafonte had a tendency, perhaps because he'd not had a strong father influence, to make father-relationships or mother-relationships with business associates. To be in a professional group with Harry was to be part of the family.

Just as Jack Rollins was instrumental in helping Belante's career take off, making his act more professional, helping Belafonte with his stage presence and his repertoire, so Kennedy can be credited with certain achievements which sent Harry's career soaring.

Kennedy obtained the Waldorf deal and a contract with the Riviera in Las Vegas. An important change in Harry's performance during Kennedy's tenure was the sexiness added to Belafonte's act. Kennedy is credited with inspiring this by some, Harry's wife by others. Harry was a dramatic singer, an emotional, outstanding performer, but he was not sexy like a Frank Sinatra. The emotions he projected were excitement, love, tension, hostility.

During this period, Kennedy and Harry changed the performer's dress style from wearing casual slacks and denims to the tight black pants that emphasized his movements. At this point he also changed his casual, open shirt to a tailored silk shirt with a plunging neckline. Harry also altered his stance and movement, becoming sexier. Perhaps this wasn't even a conscious change on Harry's part. However, his change in clothing drove the women crazy.

Just as Rollins had helped Belafonte with technique, Kennedy worked with lighting changes for more effectiveness. Pink and lavender and light blue lights emphasized sexiness rather than drama. And there were changes in pacing.

The stresses and disappointments over *Sing, Man, Sing* probably had a lot to do with the breakup between Belafonte and Kennedy. The production starred Belafonte and had the subtitle, "A New Musical Odyssey as Big as Life." Belafonte and Jay Richard Kennedy did the score, and Kennedy wrote the book and the lyrics for the production. It used a company of twenty-six.

The idea for this production came from an exhibit held at the Museum of Modern Art in 1955. It was a 500 photograph exhibit emphasizing man's relationship on a daily basis to his family, the community and to himself. The exhibition had been assembled by the famous photographer Edward Steichen. Belafonte was strongly moved by the photographs. Later the exhibit was made into a book and it was from this book and exhibit that the idea for *Sing, Man, Sing* evolved.

Involved in the production were Bill Attaway the writer, Norman Luboff, the conductor and choral director, and Lord Burgess, the calypso songwriter. However, the major share of the credit—and later the blame—went to Jay Richard Kennedy.

Several performances were given at the Academy of Music in Brooklyn in April of 1956. However, the production never reached Broadway. The story dealt with a saga in words and music of man's continual search for contentment. There was dialogue and song, including one musical number, "Eden Was Like This," which was written by Kennedy and Lord Burgess and became a favorite of Belafonte's.

The production was thought by some to be dull and pretentious. Actually, *Sing, Man, Sing* did well on the road. However, some believe this was mostly due to the fact that it was a production in which Belafonte was starring. The play was surrounded by chaos, just as Harry's life was chaotic at this time. There were more racial problems on the road.

The musical featured Harry as Man—from the Garden of Eden to modern times. It was a long trip in time, with Man searching for happiness. It featured a full orchestra, a choir, eighteen songs and even dancers, but it was still not very interesting to most. Thus the racial discrimination made the tour even more tedious. Harry was refused a room key in Baltimore because he was black. In Washington, D.C. the Daughters of the American Revolution demanded that one of the songs be left out of the production because it was immoral. There were complaints about one of the interracial dances.

Thus, *Sing, Man, Sing* was a constant headache rather than a high point of Belafonte's career. The fact that Kennedy was in so many ways responsible for this production may have had a lot to do with Belafonte's decision to fire him in September of 1956.

Another contention about the break-up between Belafonte and Kennedy is that Harry did not like Kennedy's disapproval of his relationship with Julie Robinson. If Margurite, Harry's first wife, is sometimes characterized as a mother-figure in Belafonte's life, so Kennedy has been described as a father-figure. Perhaps he was rebelling against Kennedy as a son rebels against a father when he broke his association with Kennedy and thus affirmed his relationship with Julie. Part of what a mature man does is outgrow his childhood relationship with his father. Then, his destruction of his marriage with Margurite could be seen as a destruction of a mother-son relationship, also an affirmation of maturity.

At any rate, whatever the causes, Belafonte's career took a turn for a moment. He would be soaring higher than ever in the months to come, but the flop of his musical sent him into a nose dive and he dismissed both Kennedy and his wife. Kennedy retaliated with a lawsuit which surfaced in April of 1957. Claiming that Belafonte owed him certain monies from various songs and corporations with which they were both involved, the lawsuit, if nothing else, was upsetting. Belafonte asked the court to dismiss the suit, giving his reasons. Finally, in July of 1957 the suit was discontinued by mutual agreement. The amount of money involved in a settlement has not been revealed.

However, it was not so much the money but the bother of the disagreements, coming after the poor showing of Belafonte's musical, which added to the turmoil of Harry's life. Not too long after his dismissal of Kennedy, Harry would be divorcing Margurite, making this period in his life one of turbulence. He would also be forced to answer to his black public about his marriage to a white woman, or more exactly, why he, a black, had divorced a black woman, a teacher, to marry a white woman.

Crucial Times

Out of this precarious period, Belafonte did find a man to replace Kennedy in his professional life. Phil Stein would not be given the title of manager, as Belafonte had lived through too many disappointments with managers. Instead, Stein would be a salaried employee. Phil Stein was an MCA executive who was hired by Kennedy to do the lighting for *Sing, Man, Sing*. Stein went on to produce some of Harry's TV programs as well as to function in creative and business capacities for Belafonte. He was also associate producer in Belafonte's film, *Odds Against Tomorrow*.

Lest it be thought that these were bad times altogether, it is important to note that the Lewisohn Stadium triumph was also in 1956. Belafonte, dressed in a red V-necked shirt, brought more people to the stadium than in its entire thirty-nine-year history for his concert. The interesting thing about this concert was that Harry appeared in the second half; the first half featured the New York Philharmonic Orchestra. It is reported that the Philharmonic, a popular orchestra, experienced disinterest by the public as it played. During such beautiful works as Tchaikowsky's "Romeo and Juliet," the audience could be heard conversing during the softer passages. They were waiting for Belafonte.

The *New York Times* reported that the Philharmonic "made little headway against the continuous roar of excited conversation among listeners who considered the symphonic part of the program an overlong introduction to Mr. Belafonte." This concert in the open air in a stadium that could seat 25,000 could not have been an easy one for Harry, who had just had an operation to remove nodes from his vocal cords which had caused chronic laryngitis. He had to rely solely on his voice, as the crowd in the stadium could not see the dramatic devices he used in small night clubs. Also, he was not in the best frame of mind at the time, with all of the things that were going on in his life.

The concert made entertainment history. There were people turned away, people who tried to climb the stadium walls.

The laryngitis from which Belafonte had suffered made it difficult for him to do the Lewishon Stadium concert. It had made him cancel an engagement at the Waldorf in order to have surgery. He'd suffered from chronic sinusitis and laryngitis as far back as his friends could remember. Sometimes untrained singers like Belafonte, who sing directly from the throat and larynx, contract laryngitis. Trained singers know how to project from the diaphragm in a way that they place less strain on their vocal cords.

Belafonte did not seem to feel that his laryngitis was a result of improper singing techniques. Rather, it would seem to be the medical symptom of guilt-feelings about being a star, while others were still suffering and struggling. Perhaps, then, it was a subconscious effort to fail. It was true that the laryngitis did force him to cancel many concerts. Another explanation for the laryngitis, which stopped a show in New York and again caused problems in Miami when he was supposed to sing the national anthem at a football game, could be that it was an escape device. If things got too tough, if there was a difficult decision to be made, a case of laryngitis could certainly be a rescue.

At any rate, the laryngitis began to cause problems in 1956. Perhaps it was Harry's despondence about the future after the flop of *Sing, Man, Sing*. Or maybe the problems in his marriage added the overdose of tension that caused the laryngitis to surface again. Whatever the cause, the laryngitis appeared—a very bad case—on the eve of Belafonte's appearance at the Waldorf in May.

When the doctor examined him he found nodes. The nodes on his vocal cords had been there for some time. The doctor felt they would probably go away with proper treatment. However, as the doctor couldn't guarantee the nodes would disappear without surgery, Belafonte decided to have them removed. It has been said that Harry is impatient, a person who hates waiting for answers.

Many singers, including Bing Crosby, have had surgery to remove nodes. Belafonte canceled the Waldorf engagement and entered the hospital. The operation went without incident and Harry was home in a few days. In less than a month he captured the crowd in Lewisohn Stadium.

There were many night club triumphs following the successful Lewisohn Stadium concert. July saw Belafonte at the Riviera in Las Vegas, where reviewers marveled at his ability to command the attention of the audience, even during the dinner show. In August, Belafonte again played the Palmer House in Chicago to a packed crowd. He played the Waldorf in September to a full house.

In November, while playing the Town and Country Club in Brooklyn, there was a memorable incident for Belafonte. Some of his old chums from childhood came backstage to say hello. These were white men, and Harry was able to reunite with some of the people who had caused him so much pain as a child. He remembered when he and his brother Dennis had tried to be accepted by this group by pretending to be white. They had been forced to listen to anti-Negro jokes and they'd been made to feel like outsiders. It felt good to have these men be proud of him, to hear them explain how they had been confused as children, how they hadn't really known any better when they acted like bigots.

During a triumphant booking at the Eden Roc in Miami there was another incident dealing with racial prejudice. Belafonte was asked by a publicity man to sing the national anthem at the North-South football game. Harry accepted, only to be called up the next day by the publicist, who apologized and explained that there'd been a mix up, that there were too many pre-game activities to include the national anthem.

Not willing to accept this racial slight, Harry gave the story to the papers. The eyes of the nation were now focused on the incident. Suddenly it turned out that the schedule had been wrong and that there would indeed be time for the national anthem. Harry sang the national anthem before the kickoff and then returned to his engagement at the Eden Roc. Unfortunately, whether it was because of the stress of the racial incident or because of something else, Belafonte developed laryngitis and couldn't perform that night.

Perhaps the most disconcerting event that happened during this time, and possibly the motivation behind some of the other disorder, was the decision Harry had to make about his marriage. During this time he finally made up his mind to divorce Margurite, his wife of nine years and the mother of his two daughters, in order to marry Julie Robinson. Not only was divorce stressful, but the fact that he was divorcing an educated black woman in order to marry a white woman was bound to cause problems in his relationships with other blacks. Belafonte loved his daughters and he knew that the divorce would cause his children great difficulty. This difficult decision must have weighed heavily on Belafonte.

Contrary to what one might think, since Belafonte married Julie shortly after his divorce from Margurite, the Belafonte break up does not seem to have been because of the "other woman." The things that distanced Harry from Margurite actually started when they first met in 1944. At that time Margurite and Harry were two very different kinds of people. After they married, Margurite hoped that her husband would change, become more like her and accept her values. What appears to have happened is that, although Harry got the courage through being with the strong, intelligent, middle-class Margurite to find himself, to develop an identity and a set of values, they did not turn out to be the same as Margurite's. The more self-confidence and success he acquired, the more he became himself. The self that turned out to be the mature Harry Belafonte was not compatible with Margurite and what she stood for. Julie Robinson, as a person, wanted what Harry wanted and liked the same lifestyle.

When Harry met Margurite he was poor, hostile and disturbed. He did not know what he wanted from life nor how to get it. She, on the other hand, was from a loving, middle-class family. Margurite was educated, well-read and self-confident. She knew she wanted to teach and be involved in psychology. It is said that in the early days, Harry and Margurite had a joke that he was retarded and needed her to help him.

Margurite was Harry's teacher. Being educated in psychology, she could see that his unresolved hostility at being black, at not having had a father around, etc., might turn into delinquency if he did not learn how to express it. She had long talks with him and gave him books to read about black culture and black heritage.

If she acted as a kind of teacher, then perhaps she also functioned as a type of mother, for she was more mature than Harry at the time. It has been suggested that perhaps in marrying Margurite, Harry was marrying a person who was what he'd like to be—self-confident, centered, and knowing how to deal with life. When Harry became more like this person, he didn't need a teacher anymore. Also, as a mature man, he no longer needed a mother.

As for Margurite, perhaps she married Harry hoping that as he got older he would settle down more, get rid of his belligerence. However, after their marriage, instead of looking for a profession Harry remained obsessed with becoming an actor. She was teaching at the time, providing him with a home and financial support, thus giving him security. But Harry did not move to build a home life, take on a profession. The longer they were married the more he moved away from what she'd hoped he would be.

Where he did start getting work it was singing jobs that involved traveling and thus a more irregular life. One source quotes Harry as saying of Margurite that she was a perfectly normal person who understood 8 am to

5 pm. She had high materialistic values which pressured him. His traveling for long periods of time, which was necessary to the advancement of his career, disturbed their home life. Margurite felt that Harry's career wasn't going anywhere, and he felt that she did not understand show business.

Harry did not work at building a home as Margurite understood a home to be, in the middle-class sense. Their relationship became more difficult as he began traveling. It was of extreme importance to Belafonte to make something of himself. Perhaps he took Margurite and her needs for granted, as his needs to succeed were overwhelming.

Margurite has described the difficulties of being married to a man who was not home very often. She is quoted as saying that Harry felt guilty about not being home with his family, about not being a family man. There was a period of two years when Belafonte was said to have been home for a total of six weeks. During those times Margurite would take the kids to see their dad on holidays.

It must take a certain type of spouse to be happily married to an entertainer, just as it's said that to be married to a doctor one must be a certain kind of person. Margurite did recognize how difficult the climb to success was for Harry. She saw his intense drive, his need to make it as a somebody. She expressed amazement that he became an outstanding success with all the personality problems he seemed to have. She also realized that Harry needed freedom and space in order to be the kind of performer that he wanted to be.

Although Harry was very lonely on the road, his being away from home and ultimately his divorce were in line with his basic restlessness. It's hard to get rid of patterns established in childhood. Harry lived with his grandparents in the West Indies and was boarded from house to house. Then, back in New York, life was the same. As his mother was a domestic, Harry did not really establish roots. If leaving his mother and home to join the Navy represented a kind of restlessness, perhaps leaving Margurite, who was in some ways like a mother-substitute, was yet again this restlessness. One leaves home when one has outgrown the place and the people.

In line with his basic restlessness was the irregularity and rootlessness of any entertainer's life. Perhaps this type of life was natural to Harry. However, Margurite had been brought up in a stable environment. Getting started as an actor meant working twenty-two hours one day and perhaps only four the next. There's always someplace to go to. In this kind of situation, when both parties in a relationship do not accept the lifestyle, the unorthodox hours, then damage to the relationship is inevitable. There are little things that don't seem important until finally someone realizes the relationship is sinking. Then it is sometimes too late to repair the cracks.

It has been said that Harry began to neglect Margurite, just as a boy who leaves home a lot would neglect his mother when he doesn't need her as much. Belafonte, instead of showering his attentions on his wife, gave them to his older daughter Adrienne. Then there were the women.

Perhaps the handsome performer doesn't exist who isn't besieged by women. Harry's popularity with the girls couldn't have contributed to the stability of his home life. Women throw themselves at male performers, often indiscreetly. Performers' wives often stand by while their husbands fend off brazen women. It is said that Margurite was very sensible about the women. She was a stable person and felt that Harry just needed time to mature. She would tell prying reporters that anyone in Harry's position would always be involved in rumors about women.

In spite of her tolerance, the situation must have posed problems. She spent much of their life together keeping busy. Even when she no longer needed to work she found things to do.

Another, perhaps more subtle reason for their incompatiblity was Harry's need for affection. If he has been cited as neglecting Margurite, it was also pointed out that his wife was not very demonstrative. Not having had much affection given him as a child, he craved love. There was a void in him always trying to be filled, never getting enough. The excited, applauding audiences were necessary, but they were not enough. He needed his friends to love him. His business associates had to love him and his relatives had to love him.

Margurite, being a rather reserved woman, perhaps could not fill that seemingly insatiable need. She did not fit in with the uninhibited theater and Village crowd where Harry felt comfortable. Both Harry and Margurite came to realize later that perhaps their relationship was not based on the love of a man for a woman, or the love of a woman for a man. Perhaps it really was more a mother-son relationship. Harry yearned for the things that Margurite already was when he met her. She was the image of what he wanted to be.

Margurite in retrospect could see that she had often assumed the role of protecting Harry. Perhaps her feelings for him had been more that of a mother protecting a child than a woman romantically in love with a man. If a marriage is based on a mother-son relationship, it is hard to change it, even if a wife senses that her husband has outgrown the relationship. In what is sometimes referred to as the "dance of death," one person keeps acting in such a way as to invite the treatment he has himself outgrown.

Margurite could perhaps see in retrospect that Harry had become a big man to others while still a delinquent when at home. In starting to dislike this delinquent he would start to dislike the woman who still treated him like a child.

So, the reason for the divorce was not Julie. Julie and Margurite were not competitive with one another. They were two different kinds of people. Harry's needs, his outlook and his personality at this time in his life were harmonious to those of Julie. It was not so much that Harry had changed, but more that Margurite, who had started at the opposite pole from Harry, had not changed. Harry's course had become more and more clearly defined as his career moved upward, and Margurite had not gone over to his ways. By the time Harry became interested in Julie, his relationship with Margurite was already seriously impaired.

Chapter Seven
A Divorce and a Marriage

There are several versions of when the Belafonte marriage broke up. The actual divorce wasn't until the beginning of 1957. However, some sources say that Harry requested a divorce from his wife as early as September of 1954. It was at this time that Margurite found Julie's letters to Harry. If this was true, then the divorce did not take place in 1954 because Margurite did not agree. Harry's mother also opposed her son's divorce. Margurite denies that divorce was discussed at that time. Harry was troubled about their relationship, however, and the mere idea that he was upset by the situation gave her hope that their difficulties could be solved.

After 1954 there was definitely an imbalance and a blockage in their marriage. For the marriage to have continued the couple would have had to work at bringing their relationship back to what it once was. Otherwise, with things as they were, the marriage would break up. The latter is what happened.

A picture of the couple in January, 1957, shows Margurite leaving for Vegas, where she obtained the divorce. Margurite looked anguished in the photo, and Harry seemed to be pleading to be left alone by the photographers. Their marriage was just short of being nine years old when the divorce was granted. According to Harry, the marriage had been over for a long time. He felt the agreement to separate came in the early months of 1956. She seemed to feel that their decision to break up didn't come until September of 1956.

In September of 1956 Margurite went on a tour of the West Indies alone. Harry set up a bachelor apartment on the West Side in the city. Perhaps Harry didn't move completely out of the Elmhurst house at this time, but he did take a separate place of residence.

Several other things suggested that Belafonte had decided to break with his wife early in 1956. He organized a publishing company under the name of Clara Music. Julie's mother was named Clara. Pictures on his record albums at the time show that Belafonte was extremely distressed. If one compares Belafonte's eager, thrilling look on the *Calypso* LP jacket to the *Belafonte* album which was released in 1956, the trouble and unhappiness can be seen.

At one point Margurite stated that their actual decision to divorce was not made until the day she left for Las Vegas. Later she stated that it might have only seemed that way. At the time of Belafonte's divorce, Julie was already several months pregnant with his

A Divorce and a Marriage

child. It would seem that perhaps Belafonte was more sure of his decision to divorce and then remarry than Margurite knew.

However, it is certain that in September of 1956, the couple did separate. Margurite toured the Caribbean, modeling clothes. She was part of a group known as the Brandford Goodwill Tour. She was supposed to be using this time of separation to make up her mind what to do, just as Harry was doing the same. One source reported that some of the clothing modeled by Margurite had been selected by Harry. Another source stated that Margurite received several letters a week from her husband while she was traveling.

At any rate, the divorce discussions did start when Margurite returned to New York. The news of the split was known, for Belafonte did not receive an award that was to be given him. The James J. Hoey Award for Interracial Justice, an award given by the Catholic Interracial Council, was withdrawn.

In January, Margurite left for Las Vegas. A story written at the time by the *Pittsburgh Courier* described the breakup of the Belafontes as "strange." The breakup was strange because, according to reports, Margurite and Harry only said nice things about each other. It was also stated that Harry had persuaded Margurite to delay her trip to Nevada for a week. It was also stated that Harry and Margurite dined together, and that Harry babysat while Margurite had business engagements. There was also the matter of all the presents he had given her, including a white mink for Christmas.

At the time of the divorce, Margurite was quoted as saying she had great admiration for Harry. She didn't

BELAFONTE

deny that she'd been hurt, but felt that perhaps she would have reacted in a similar way as Belafonte, had she met with great success. He suddenly found people at his feet, and in that case, wasn't it hard to be strong? He was not so much a bad person, then, as a victim of circumstances.

He was still attentive and certainly devoted to the children, according to Margurite at this time. It was reported that Belafonte showered Margurite with parting gifts of a $10,000 diamond and sapphire bracelet, a white mink and a $2500 opal and diamond ring.

According to Margurite, the six weeks residence was a difficult period. During the last two weeks of the period, Harry, the two children and a nurse were all there. Although she went to Vegas by herself, leaving Harry in New York, Belafonte was booked in California. He had the kids with him. For the last two weeks they were all in Vegas, as Harry was playing the Riviera.

She received flowers from him during this time. He made sure she had a car at her disposal, and saw that she had a comfortable place to stay. On the day of the divorce he kept the kids, taking pictures and trying to cheer them up. Adrienne, the eldest, was troubled by the divorce.

There are numerous stories about the size and content of the divorce settlement. All of them seem to indicate that the settlement was generous, although the actual amount has not been made public. On the 28th of February, Margurite was a free woman, with the custody of the Belafonte daughters.

It was reported that the reality of what had happened did not hit Margurite until she returned to Elmhurst.

A Divorce and a Marriage

Margurite was a beautiful, composed, strong woman. Probably because she had been maintaining her dignity throughout the divorce proceedings, she did not really feel the pain. She found herself unable to eat, powerless to prevent the depression. It is possible that Margurite was trying to become the kind of woman Harry wanted. As a person she felt worthless, and was perhaps subconsciously trying to destroy herself. At least, that is what one source is quoted as hearing her say.

However, Margurite was an intelligent, active woman. With extreme will power she was able to bring herself out of the depression, to eat again. She cut her hair short, symbolic of a determination not to be like Julie. The ultimate result of the divorce was a strengthening of herself. Just as Harry had needed to destroy the mother-son relationship in order to be a mature man, so Margurite needed to get out of her back seat role as a person.

During her marriage to Harry she had to come second, so that Harry could have the limelight. She was of help to him, assisting him in channeling his anger into social directions as well as professional ones. Now Margurite began to use her intelligence to step forward herself. The divorce provoked her into an advance into the public eye. She now developed social drive.

As a married woman, Margurite thought of herself mainly as a mother and a housewife. As a matter of fact, she often resented having to work when their marriage was in its early stages, because she couldn't stay home. Now, as a free woman with financial security, she became active in the NAACP, among other organizations. In 1959, as a fund raiser for the NAACP, she visited 168 cities. Once, when Congressman Adam Clayton Powell of Harlem was in the hospital, he was asked about possible successors to himself. One of the people he named as a potentially competent candidate was Margurite Belafonte.

If Margurite eventually became stronger and more productive as a result of the divorce, there was still Harry's older daughter who would suffer. Not only would the divorce trouble Adrienne, requiring her to undergo therapy, but Harry himself felt badly about the divorce because of its effect on his child.

Harry, as do many fathers, had a very close, strong relationship with his first daughter. Much of Belafonte's unhappiness about the divorce is thought to have stemmed from his feelings for Adrienne and how she would feel about the separation of her parents. Some first daughters become an outlet for affection when the father does not give this affection to his wife. There are pictures of Adrienne as a little girl wearing a belt whose buckle was a smaller version of the one worn by Harry during performances.

There are pictures of the two of them, showing how much Harry cared for his daughter. When Belafonte was on the road, it is reported that he always found gifts for Adrienne if not for his wife. It was observed that Adrienne was the one upon whom Harry showered his affection, not Margurite, his wife.

When Belafonte faced divorce, he had to think of the adverse effect it would have on Adrienne. Even when they were separated in 1956, he went home frequently so as not to upset his daughter. Perhaps that is why the separation was not really known—Harry and Margurite

A Divorce and a Marriage

didn't want an open break that would hurt their daughter. Harry said in an article that talking about the divorce with his daughter was very difficult. Even when he decided to remarry, his concern was how this would affect his daughter.

In spite of the guilt, the pain and the tension of divorce, Harry Belafonte, a little over a week after his divorce from Margurite, was married to Julie Robinson. Although news of the marriage did not get out until April, Julie and Harry became man and wife on March 8, 1957. Belafonte is reported to have kept the marriage secret for about a month in order to spare his daughter. He planned to tell her when she visited him during her Easter vacation.

Harry's marriage to Julie made for difficulties not only because it would shock his children, but also because he was divorcing a black woman in order to marry a white one. This move could hurt him for two reasons; Harry, as a black who fought for civil rights and equality, could be seen as failing his people, and his divorce and quick remarriage could affect his status as a star.

The marriage took place in Mexico. On March 8, Harry left Las Vegas, where he was in the midst of an engagement, and flew to San Diego. Picking up Julie and her parents, he motored across the border into Tecate. There, in a civil ceremony, they became man and wife. Then Harry drove back to San Diego and flew to Las Vegas in time for his concert that night. For five more days he played to a full house, with no one guessing that he had remarried.

After the Vegas engagement he picked Julie up in Los Angeles and the couple flew to New York. For almost a month Julie stayed in Harry's bachelor apartment without the press guessing that Belafonte had a new wife. The announcement to the press was made on April 9th. On the 22nd of April Julie first appeared in public with Harry as the new Mrs. Belafonte.

Naturally, during the month before the marriage announcement was made public, there were rumors and attempts by the press to find out the truth. Even while Margurite was getting the divorce in Las Vegas there was gossip that Harry was seeing Julie on a regular basis.

There was also talk about Julie as a person. She, a small, dark woman with long braids, was often said to be part Indian. Sometimes when the press was too annoying, Harry encouraged the rumor. There would be much more talk about Harry's relationship with a white woman as the marriage became known.

Many papers and reporters attempted to break the story of Harry's possible marriage. One paper wrote that Harry was still carrying a torch for Margurite. There is another instance where a paper reported that Harry and two prominent men from Harlem (a politician and a musician) had stayed up all night discussing Harry's possible attempt at reconciliation with Margurite. Apparently, while the two men were trying to talk Harry into going back with his wife, he did not tell them he had already remarried.

The news finally leaked out before Harry could break the news to his daughter. Supposedly, a reporter posing as a census taker had rung the Belafonte doorbell. When Julie answered he had asked to speak with Mrs. Belafonte, and she had replied that she was Mrs. Belafonte.

A Divorce and a Marriage

At any rate, Harry's office made a formal announcement about the Mexican marriage on April 9.

The newspapers had a field day with the news of the marriage. While the *New York Times* carried a single paragraph giving simple details of the marriage, the *Amsterdam News* ran a story on its front page. The headline ran, BELAFONTE WEDS WHITE DANCER. The interracial issue of the marriage became big news. The other issue was noted in a caption of the *Amsterdam News* on April 20—"WILL HARRY'S MARRIAGE AFFECT HIS STATUS AS MATINEE IDOL?"

Belafonte had to deal with both of these questions. One paper, focusing on the intermarriage, accused Belafonte of being unfair by shedding a black for a white. Belafonte, who had suffered and fought discrimination from whites, was now to have problems with blacks. The question was raised as to why a man who had supposedly fought for justice for his race would turn from a black wife to a white one.

Another article in a paper pictured Belafonte with a piece of African sculpture and also with a cultural book about blacks. This was to establish that Harry had racial pride. However, the critical article made the remark about when you give a black man fame and fortune, then he has to have a white woman. One article suggested that Belafonte's popularity with his own race was questionable.

Articles published at the time pointed out that Belafonte had problems with women, especially since he had become successful. In 1956 Belafonte had made a film in which he played a romantic lead opposite a white woman (*Island in the Sun* with Joan Fontaine); mention was, of course, made of this in relation to his marriage to a white woman.

At this point there were certainly problems between Harry and his race because of the intermarriage. For one thing, blacks are strong on family ties. Also, since teachers are highly respected in black communities, Harry's divorcing a black teacher was a double stigma.

Belafonte had to do something in order to explain his actions, not only to his people but to his public. In July, 1957, a first-person article by Harry Belafonte appeared in *Ebony*. The article was entitled, "Why I Married Julie."

Belafonte stated in the article that the marriage had nothing to do with his feelings about integration. He said he believed in integration and worked for it. However, he had only married Julie because he loved her. She had married him for the same reason—love.

Harry related the story of his meeting with Julie. According to him, he had first met her in 1947, before his marriage to Margurite. When he was attending classes at The Dramatic Workshop, a group of Katherine Dunham dancers came to his class for a demonstration. Among these girls was the pig-tailed Julie Robinson, who was a teacher at the Dunham School of Dance and Theater.

Although he found her charming and attractive at the time, he never saw her again until they met in 1954. When he met her the second time, during the filming of his picture, he found they had much to talk about. They had, of course, their common interest in the arts. They also had a common concern in the struggle of blacks for equal rights. They also had analysis in common; Julie had been in analysis and Harry was just beginning his.

In the article Belafonte explained that their conversations had developed in many directions. He had found Julie to be an animated conversationalist and was quite impressed with her. He related how, when he had met Julie's parents at this time, he was moved by their cordiality. They received him very warmly.

At this same time, according to Belafonte in the *Ebony* article, his marriage to Margurite was starting to fall apart. He felt the blame was partially his, as his work kept him away from home for long periods. Although he could keep in touch with his daughter, his marriage suffered during these absences. He said that their relationship deteriorated so much that he and Margurite knew they were unhappy.

However, instead of separating when they knew their marriage was bad, they stayed together for a while for the sake of the children. A second daughter was born in 1954. Both Margurite and Harry, concerned over the effect a separation would have on their older daughter Adrienne, tried to work out their differences. In the article Belafonte said that he loved Adrienne very much and did not want to cause her pain. When the couple finally did separate in 1956, Belafonte wrote that he frequently went to the Elmhurst house to see Adrienne.

As to his courtship with Julie, Belafonte said that it took place in California and New York. Julie came east to teach dance in Manhattan. He and Julie attended concerts, theater and ballet performances together. They also spent time in jazz clubs, art galleries and museums. As they both loved Italian cooking, they ate in Italian restaurants.

Belafonte stated in the article that his friendship with

Julie did not become intense until long after his separation from Margurite. He said they did not become really close until about six months before they were married, and that they did not talk about marriage until September of 1956.

At this point, Belafonte stated, Margurite and he had reached an understanding to divorce. This was around October of 1956. He was given the task of telling the children. Belafonte claimed that explaining the divorce to his seven-year-old Adrienne was extremely difficult. However, because the child could see that he and Margurite were civilized with one another, he felt that the impact on Adrienne wasn't too traumatic.

In the article Harry stated that he did not propose to Julie until the day of his divorce, at which time he called her and asked her to marry him. She accepted the following day. He explained that they delayed announcing the marriage because of his desire to prepare his daughter for the news.

Next, in the article Belafonte talked about Julie's background so that *Ebony* readers would know that she was very much involved with blacks and their struggle for equal rights. Upon meeting her in Hollywood, he had been very impressed by her knowledge about blacks and their problems. Also, the fact that Julie had attended mixed schools and received a liberal upbringing by her parents was important to him. Julie's people, too, had resisted injustice all their lives.

Harry told *Ebony* readers about Julie's association with the black dance company, the Katherine Dunham dancers. She spent six years with the troupe as a dancer and three as a teacher. Whenever the group encountered racial prejudice, Julie stayed with the black women to share their humiliations. There was a time in Las Vegas when the dancers had been forced to stay in a slum area. Julie did not desert them just because she was white.

Belafonte described a time in Argentina, where Julie submitted to Jim Crow with the others, rather than separate herself from the dance group. At this time the black dancers had been discriminated against in restaurants. Julie knew from first-hand experience, according to Belafonte, what it was like to be black.

Then, nearing the end of the article, Belafonte described what it was about Julie as a person that made her a good mate for him. It has been said that Harry was subject to moods. Julie was known to be a very energetic, life-affirming person. Her vivacity and animation was a good balance to Harry's lows. Margurite's reserved personality could not combat Harry's downs, because she was reserved and withdrawn.

Another one of Julie's positive additions to the relationship was her love of show business. She was known to have the entertainer's excitement at discovering new talent. Harry could turn to her for ideas; she could get excited about new record albums, new shows, etc. Margurite did not share Harry's love of show business.

In the *Ebony* article Harry talked about the fact that he was a moody man. He explained that Julie challenged his moods, rather than giving in to them, and that her understanding of him as a person was something he had long needed. Julie was able to understand and deal with the pressures of Harry's profession.

Finally, at the end of the article, Belafonte talked

about the money he was making as an entertainer. He could be of help to the NAACP, not only by contributing money, but by using his talent to fight for the freedom of blacks. He wanted very much to work for racial equality in America.

Belafonte indicated that he had just signed a million dollar contract with RCA Victor Records, which would give him $100,000 a year for the next ten years. Also, he had a four-year contract with the Riviera Hotel in Las Vegas; he would receive $560,000 for working one month a year at the Riviera. He was also in the process of negotiating a three-picture deal with Twentieth-Century Fox. (He later decided instead to make his own films.) This would be used in part to help his people.

Harry told *Ebony* readers that he would be a very busy man, but with Julie by his side he would be a happy man. It is reported, however, that in spite of Julie, Belafonte was back in analysis a few weeks after his secret remarriage.

The reaction to Harry's article was mixed. However, it seems that he got more approval than disapproval. *Ebony* ran some of the letters it received. One of the unfavorable letters printed in the September, 1957 issue suggested that this was a typical story of the man who becomes successful and drops the woman who stood by him while he climbed the ladder of success. One reader felt that it was innocent children who would suffer and that Harry's conscience would bother him.

One positive letter from a black stated that he was not opposed to their marriage, and that Harry's article had shown how love can conquer all.

Margurite Belafonte wrote a letter which was published in *Ebony*. She accused Harry of going back on an agreement they had about not making their whole story public. She also disagreed with the facts as reported by Belafonte. According to Margurite, if Harry only thought of marrying Julie on February 28th, then how could he explain the fact that she was already three months pregnant by this time. Margurite also said that Harry's newfound happiness was at the expense of his eight-year-old daughter. The daughter Harry claimed to love so much was at that moment receiving psychiatric care.

What seemed to bother the ex-wife was that *Ebony* was a magazine widely read by blacks, and Harry's version of the facts were not the same as what Margurite had endured. She had tried to be reasonable about the divorce by keeping her feelings out of the newspapers, only to have Belafonte write an article on the divorce for *Ebony*. She had to let people know that Harry's version of the story was only one side; both she and her daughter had received a lot of pain as the result of the situation.

If the divorce was traumatic at first to Margurite Belafonte, as stated earlier, she came out of it a stronger woman. She was to use her new energies to do many things. Today, Margurite Belafonte has a Ph.D. in psychology. When her self-confidence started to return, she became involved in life. Margurite went on to become a woman's page editor of a newspaper and to have a radio program. She played a part in a movie. She went on lecture tours and did some modeling. As a firm supporter of the NAACP, she was a fund raiser. Thus the divorce, and the need to be busy so as not to be hostile or blaming of other people, forced her to become active and involved.

As for Harry, his remarriage did not seem to hurt his popularity. In the summer of 1957 he toured the U.S. He was well-received and praised. As a folk singer and balladeer he was considered to be the best.

Belafonte has also been of service to his people. He has fought for desegregation and against discrimination. Belafonte took part in several youth marches for integration to Washington. He has spoken in behalf of the NAACP and contributed his time to help in the fight for justice and equal rights. Belafonte received the Brotherhood Award from the National Conference of Christians and Jews. Margurite and Harry jointly received an award for their work with children from Mizrachi, the Jewish welfare organization. In 1957 Belafonte went on a Prayer Pilgrimage for Integration to Washington.

Thus, in spite of the unpleasantness of divorce and remarriage, Belafonte and his ex-wife Margurite continued to be useful as citizens and as blacks fighting for their people. Also, if attendance and reviews are any indication, Belafonte's popularity did not suffer. As a matter of fact it was in 1957, the year of Belafonte's divorce and remarriage, that his *Calypso* album became a best seller, catapulting Harry to world fame.

Chapter Eight
King of Calypso

The professional life of Harry Belafonte is amazing if one remembers that he wanted to be an actor. He is an actor, having made many films, and he also has produced movies. However, it was as a singer, a calypso singer, that he was to become a star, a "matinee idol." His stardom really reached a peak in 1957 with the sensational success of the *Calypso* album, cut in 1955. Nevertheless, the longevity of his success as a singer is truly amazing. In 1976, twenty years later, *Variety* listed Belafonte as having made a million dollars on a European singing tour.

Harry was not at all interested in being type-cast as a calypso singer, as this was only one of his interests. He sang folk songs from all countries and times, as well as being both a stage actor and a film actor. However, the album of calypso songs sold over a million and a half copies. Harry became a sought after singer, a matinee idol. He played to packed houses in Europe as well as in the United States.

Calypso became a craze, a fad. American cities had calypso night clubs, the young did a dance called The Chalypso. Of course, the craze died down eventually, but it was an astonishing turn of events, considering that Belafonte did not consider himself just a calypso singer.

It is said that Harry practically woke up one morning to find himself an international singing star. This was in 1957, in the midst of his lawsuits with his third manager, and while his marriage was breaking up and he was preparing to marry a white woman.

He had before this time been able to show that he was the first folk singer in history to command a mass audience. He had played to record crowds at the Copa, at Lewisohn Stadium, at the Riviera, the Greek Theater in Los Angeles and at the Waldorf. Still, in 1957 he would become the first black matinee idol, being thrust into an international entertainment scene and becoming a million-dollar performer.

The album responsible for this success was cut in 1955. In 1957, having been released in the fall of '56, it became a best seller. It became the first RCA Victor LP by a single artist to sell over a million copies. It remained a best seller for over a year and a half. That is how Belafonte, in spite of himself, became the King of Calypso.

He told reporters at the time that his two best-selling records were not even calypso. "Jamaica Farewell" was

King of Calypso

a West Indian ballad and "Day-O, Banana Boat" was a West Indian work song. Belafonte stated that he was a singer, period. He was not interested in being cultish.

Belafonte, his managers and his associates did much research and reshaping of songs from all times and areas in order to get Harry's interesting repertoire compiled. Calypso, which happened to become a rage, was only a small part of the repertoire. Actually calypso is said to have come from Trinidad, an island off the coast of Venezuela in the West Indies.

Calypso is said to have first been sung in African and later in a French dialect. Then it spread to the other islands of the West Indies and at the turn of the century came into English. The origin of the calypso is very interesting, and understanding it will help us better understand Belafonte. It is thought that like American blues, it originated as a work song. As slaves weren't allowed to talk as they worked in the sugar fields, they sang. In the 18th century, the blacks in Trinidad, while their Spanish overseers looked on, sang in their native tongues. The rhythm of the songs increased productivity, so no one forbade their singing. As the Spanish could not understand their African tongues, the slaves were able to converse, gossip, complain, even plan revolts as they sang.

This set the stage for calypso. There was a lead voice, the "chantwelle," who was answered by the gangs, in the form of verse-chorus or question-answer form. When the slaves were freed in Trinidad in 1838, the tradition had already been set. By then the singing was in French. Instead of slaves, the work-gang leader was the "chantwelle." He eventually traveled from one plantation to another and made up songs about important topics, his experiences and other information. Eventually these lead singers started to compete with one another at carnival time. The calypso tradition is still today a part of life in Trinidad.

There is a professional group of calypso singers in Trinidad. Once a year they consider new applicants. The applicant must invent lyrics on the spot about any subject. Calypso songs in Trinidad must be funny and they must rhyme. Also, true calypso singers have funny, regal-sounding names such as Lord Invader, Duke of Iron and Lord Flea. There is a calypso war in which calypso singers vie for the title of King of Calypso. In order to win they try to out-do each other. The winner is the one who most sarcastically and wittily insults his competitors. They can say any terrible thing they want about each other.

One of the criticisms of calypso, when Belafonte was singing it, was that it was vulgar. Belafonte, who likes things to be real, refused to change the material. He claimed that every form of art has some blue material in it, even Shakespeare. Belafonte and his writers did change calypso songs to suit American audiences and taste. He did not claim to be singing calypso exactly as it was sung in the West Indies.

His contact with calypso material went back to when he was a lonely boy, roaming the streets and beaches of Kingston. According to Harry and others, Jamaica, having no real means of communication, related through singing. This singing became a part of Harry before he was in his teens.

Although Belafonte was to sing calypso with a variety

King of Calypso

of musical accompaniment, the original calypso was accompanied by drums. However, when these drums were outlawed in the 19th century because they sounded like war noises, singers started beating on the ground with poles. When these poles started being used in gang wars and crimes, they too were banned. Eventually, during World War II, the steel drums that we know as calypso instruments came into use. They were drums for petroleum which had been altered and were sometimes hung around the neck. Belafonte uses original sounding instruments for calypso as well as jazz music to give different sounds.

The actual *Calypso* album came about as a result of a TV show. Harry was to do a show, "Holiday in Trinidad," for the *Colgate Comedy Hour*. He collaborated with Bill Attaway and Lord Burgess in the preparation of the score for the 1955 show. The "Banana Boat Song" was heard by American audiences for the first time on this show.

After the show, Belafonte started recording some of the songs for a new album for RCA Victor. Harry, overscheduled as usual, having just completed a successful but tiring engagement at The Waldorf and preparing to leave the state for another engagement, recorded the most successful album of his career. Not only was "The Banana Boat Song" in the album, but also Lord Burgess had just written "Jamaica Farewell." Burgess adapted this song from a Caribbean folk tune, changing the lyric and slowing down the melody. "Banana Boat" and "Jamaica Farewell" became hit singles.

As previously stated, two years later the *Calypso* album became a smash. Belafonte had recorded calypso songs before 1955, and so had other singers in America. No one knows why at one time some form of music or some song is not a hit, and at another, it might be a smash. There was a man, Wilmuth Houdini, who made calypso recordings before World War I. He had a hit, "Stone Cold Dead in the Market." In 1944, Morey Amsterdam had a best seller called "Rum and Coca-Cola." The Andrews Sisters made this last song a million-copy best seller calypso.

Belafonte recorded "Matilda, Matilda" in 1953. In 1954 he recorded several calypso numbers—"Hole 'Em Joe" and "Man Piaba"—but the public was not ready for calypso. Nevertheless, by 1957 his calypso album was a million-copy best seller.

Even though Belafonte is credited with being the cause of the calypso craze in the Fifties, there were other calypso songs and singers at that time. The Tarriers made a hit, "Cindy, Oh Cindy," which had a Caribbean touch. They also made a recording of the "Banana Boat Song," but it was Belafonte's that sold, not only in the States but in Europe.

Rosemary Cloney recorded "Mangoes, Papaya." "Marianne" was also a big selling calypso number, but its singer, Terry Gilkyson, did not achieve identification as an interterpreter of calypso.

So, Harry was the King of Calypso, the one who was to tour the world singing calypso, as well as other songs, to packed houses. He had to answer to the allegation that calypso songs were dirty. His answer was that he would always sing true calypso as he saw it, just as he would sing every other kind of music that had truth in it. The original calypso is humorous, crazily accented and frequently bawdy. There was also controversy over whether Belafonte sang authentic calypso, although Belafonte had never claimed to sing authentic calypso. He had to simplify it to make it acceptable for American listening. As an artist, he was adding a new dimension to the original calypso which he had known as a boy. He changed the calypso so that it would reflect the dignity, the humanness and the tenderness of the people who originally sang the songs.

Calypso became a rage, the hit songs making Belafonte sought after as a performer not only in the U.S. but in Europe, where the calypso songs were extremely popular. Belafonte not only had a hit record album at this time. He had made a film in 1956 which was released in 1957. This film was very controversial because Belafonte played a romantic lead opposite a white star. He was the first American black to play a romantic role in a feature film opposite a major white actress.

Island In The Sun starred Belafonte and Joan Fontaine. The interesting fact is that Harry made this film just before he himself became the center of controversy among blacks because he married a white girl. In the film, however, the couple decides not to marry at the end.

Depending on which critic one reads, the film is either stunning or not so good. It did well at the box office, which is at least one indication of success. There was no disagreement about the beauty of the setting of *Island In The Sun*. The scenic lush of Barbados, with its shimmering houses, green hills, crowded harbor and exquisite shots of the sea, is the dominant beauty of the film. The film, in Cinemascope and color, portrays the stunning aspects of the West Indian island, which are enough to set the moviegoer longing to fly away to the eternal sun of Barbados.

The film, based on a novel by Alec Waugh, weaves many narrative threads into the story as written for the screen by Alfred Hayes. James Mason plays an estate owner who is married to Patricia Owens. Mason, who is insecure for reasons that go back in his life, is also very jealous of his wife. He suspects her of being romantically involved with Hillary Carson, played by Michael Rennie. In a burst of anger Mason kills Rennie. Next there is a game of wits between Mason and the police. Mason finally confesses.

Then there is the story of David Boyer, played by Harry Belafonte. Boyer, a man of smoldering emotional drive, is a labor leader seeking freedom for his people and power for himself. He falls in love with Joan Fontaine, who plays a white socialite on the island. Their love cannot jump over the color line obstacles in order to reach fulfillment. But John Justin, a white aide to the governor of the island, falls in love with a beautiful native, Dorothy Dandridge. They do succeed, after some problems, in getting married and leaving for England. There is another successful romance in the film, that of Mason's sister, played by Joan Collins, and Stephen Boyd, as the governor's son. In the film Joan Collins thinks she has colored blood, but when she finds out that she doesn't, she is able to be married.

As one critic noted, the film had enough stories for several films. Belafonte's role of a belligerent fighter for black rights is opposite Joan Fontaine's aristocratic character. The two of them, though in love, decide that marriage would only mean snubs and misery. When *Ebony* ran an article about the film it was in the same issue as the article by Belafonte on why he'd married Julie.

The first two films in which Belafonte had appeared were essentially all-black casts. *Carmen Jones* had been all-black, and *The Bright Road* had included only one white actor. *Island In The Sun* involved two interracial relationships. This movie dealt with the problems of intermarriage on two levels: the white man who loves a black woman and the black man who loves a white woman. Harry was said to have not been too impressed by the role he was to play; however, he felt that the theme of the movie was important enough for him to do the film. The movie was based on a best-selling novel, and the film did good business.

It was a daring production for Hollywood. Not only did Belafonte have a daring role in this film because he loved a white woman, but his role as a trade union leader who beat a white man in a heavy political battle was avant garde. Another interesting element of the film's story was Maxwell Fleury's (Mason) belief that he had Negro blood in his aristocratic family.

Belafonte sang two songs in *Island In The Sun*, reflecting the Caribbean flavor of the film. Both songs, "Island in the Sun" and "Lead Man Holler," appear in his record album, *Belafonte Sings of the Caribbean*.

One person praised Belafonte's performance as a remarkable combination of violence and sensitivity, with an added ability to communicate with the audience. One scene, in which Belafonte spoke non-stop for five minutes on the economic and social problems of blacks in his town, was shot and printed after only one take, remarkable for the film business.

It is said that early in 1956, when Belafonte had completed the film, he felt he was reaching his original goal, that of being an actor. Unfortunately, although the film did good box office, neither Belafonte nor the film received good overall reviews. One critic did not feel that the subject of race had been dealt with successfully. Even though the film dealt with racial conflict, it did not reach any conclusions.

One critic really did not think much of any of the performances. He suggested that Harry was aggressive without persuasiveness of purpose. He found Joan Fontaine hazy and meaningless as a young widow who followed Belafonte around. He found Joan Collins and Stephen Boyd rather wan in their portrayal of a vapid love affair. Also he wrote that Dorothy Dandridge and John Justin were ineffectual in their roles. Another critic attacked the film as lacking in courage. He stated that although Belafonte was extremely good-looking, in the film he was heroic and bronzelike rather than real. And still another critic found the film good in its candid treatment of the racial issue, but he found Belafonte rather slow and sleepy.

Belafonte is reported to have been angry about the reviews. One report states that Harry accused his first film, *The Bright Road*, of being too bland, and *Island In The Sun* of being a horrible picture based on a bad book. Part of the explanation by one critic for the film's failure to achieve greatness was the fact that the screenwriter had not been able to assemble the elements of the multi-character and multi-plot book. Even though several characters were dropped, the screenwriter had not been able to give the moviegoer a clear and integrated account of the trouble in Santa Marta.

This critic found that the picture was lacking a precise and confident theme. If the film pretended to be scanning racial problems, it presented them in a vague way, the observations were fuzzy and no conclusions were reached. The critic described the beginning of the film as starting with several intimations of racial issues and hostilities. Then these intimations are left hanging while the picture goes along to be concerned about Mason's concern over his black blood. Then, claims the critic, the Mason race thing is put aside while Mason stops to murder the English bachelor out of sheer jealousy. The murder had nothing to do with racial conflict.

Then, in conclusion, it is suggested that—as was the case with *Pinky*, also produced by Darryl Zanuck—*Island In The Sun* did not present a frank, unembarrassed and conclusive grappling with the subject of race.

Harry is said to have brought up the fact that his films had been compromised, just as his singing career was a compromise. When the chance came to act in *Porgy and Bess*, Belafonte turned it down. Just as he had refused to continue as a pop-jazz singer, doing songs whose words meant nothing to him, he refused to be in a film of which he did not approve.

Porgy had a budget of seven million dollars and top stars like Sidney Poitier, Sammy Davis, Jr. and Pearl Bailey. The musical score was by George Gershwin. Yet, as Belafonte had guessed, the film encountered considerable criticism among blacks. *Porgy* exposed certain unfavorable images of blacks at a time when blacks were fighting for equality. If the film portrayed impoverished blacks, that was one thing; but the leading lady was a prostitute, a leading male character was a pusher, and the hero a cripple.

While *Island In The Sun* was being filmed, the relationships between cast members of different races was said to have been pleasant. Any problems which developed within the cast were personal rather than racial. Harry was accused of pretentiousness, of constantly mentioning scholarly books and using words of many syllables. The one racial "problem" was that Belafonte was asked by the producers not to refer to Joan Fontaine in any public statements. It seems there were those who were trying to publicize a mixed affair between Harry and Joan.

If there were no racial problems encountered among the cast, there were repercussions with the public. The producers of the film were careful not to have Belafonte and Fontaine kiss in the movie. They were, however, allowed to drink from the same coconut together in one scene.

Joan Fontaine received hate letters, and demands were made that the film not be shown to the armed forces. In South Carolina, there was a bill introduced into the legislature to fine any theater that showed the film $5,000. The producer, Darryl F. Zanuck, announced that he would pay the fine for any theater showing the film. A representative in South Carolina called the film sickening and indecent. In Virginia there was a similar protest. The film was considered by some as revolting to the sensibilities of an overwhelming majority of the citizens. Warning was made that the film could lead to racial disturbances.

King of Calypso

Filmmakers and film actors and actresses had to expect those kinds of criticism during the early years of racial changes in films and all arts. Black singers who sang with white bands and white singers who sang with black bands had to endure criticism in order to pave the way for integration in the arts. The Italian film *La Dolce Vita* was banned in many areas in the United States because people of more than one race were pictured riding in a convertible.

Nevertheless, this prejudice could not have been fun for Belafonte or any of those concerned. At around the same time as the release of *Island In The Sun*, it was told that Belafonte was refused an apartment because of his color. When the landlord found out from his wife and daughter who Harry Belafonte was, he asked him to move into his building. This time it was Belafonte who refused.

If it was true that Belafonte was subjected to reproach for playing in an interracial film by his own people, then it is also true that as a "matinee idol" he did much to further the cause of integration and acceptance of blacks. Before the advent of Belafonte as a matinee idol, a black was only accepted by whites as attractive or romantic if he did not look black. If you were black but looked white, it was acceptable. It is said that Harry represented the next stage in public acceptance of blacks; he was definitely black because his skin was dark, but he had a handsomeness that was appealing to whites. His features were acceptable because they weren't pronounced Negroid. The next stage of public acceptance would be Sidney Poitier, who, although not considered handsome in the Caucasian sense of the word, was beautiful as a black.

Perhaps it was not so important that blacks at the time weren't approving of Belafonte's marriage. The need was for a black who could bridge the gap in the struggle for human freedom. Belafonte, because his looks were acceptable to whites and because he was also definitely black, filled the need. This might indicate in part Harry's phenomenal rise to fame at this time. The timidity of the American integration movement had created a need for Harry's widespread acceptance as a matinee idol.

There are few singers and actors who have become sex symbols and love gods to American women, although there have been many men who have become extremely successful as actors and singers. Today there is Burt Reynolds and there is Robert Redford. Yesterday there was Rudolph Valentino, Rudy Vallee and Clark Gable. Of course there was Elvis and there is Frank Sinatra. However, there are not too many men who have become famous matinee idols. Harry Belafonte is one.

His good looks, dynamic bearing and movements are some of the reasons women went crazy when Belafonte was on stage. His hostility was another. Marlon Brando and James Dean also had this hostile quality that made them appealing to women. Perhaps Harry's hostility started as that of a proud black reacting to white prejudice. Whatever the reason for it, women find it attractive in a male.

The movie publicists and newspapers took up the title, "Negro matinee idol," for Belafonte. Even though he was not overwhelmed with acceptance by blacks at this period, his career was growing by leaps and bounds. When he played at the Coconut Grove in Los Angeles,

King of Calypso

he brought the biggest crowds he had ever attracted to the nightclub. In July, during an engagement at the Greek Theater in Hollywood, he set a new record. Even then, when his remarriage was a controversial issue, he filled the 4,400 seat open-air theater, taking in $84,500 during one week.

It was said that during this year Belafonte was going to reach the one million dollar income level. Not only was he making more money than ever before, but also Belafonte was being written up and reviewed in some of the big magazines. Thus he was to change in 1957 from the status of well-known artist to celebrity. In April of 1957, *The Saturday Evening Post* published a long story on Belafonte. Also at this time *The New York Post* ran a week-long serial on his life and career. *Look* ran a long feature story on Belafonte at this time, and *Life* published a picture story on him. *Time Magazine* also devoted its music section to Belafonte.

All of these publications agreed that it was true Belafonte had become a matinee idol. One female newspaper columnist wrote that he was handsome as sin, as well as being romantic because of his West Indian background.

That Harry was the first "Negro matinee idol" in the history of the United States was a reflection of the change in Americans. Even if Belafonte did not like the title given to him, just as he did not like being typecast, it represented a positive move in the direction of equality for all races. It is said, however, that Belafonte liked the title "Negro matinee idol" even less than that of "King of Calypso." He did not think of himself as pitching to women especially, in spite of the fact that there were always women tearing down his posters when he was performing.

It was also said that while Belafonte was not a playboy, he was very conscious of his appeal to women. If he worked at being a charmer, it reflected his need for love. It's a reaction dating back to his youth when he felt unloved, without roots. His need, then, was not for romance as much as positive response from people.

Chapter Nine
From Surgery to Stardom

During 1957 Belafonte had the horrendous experience of almost losing his eyesight, or possibly being cross-eyed. However, in 1958, after three operations, the eye problem was permanently corrected and Belafonte went on not only to record a blues album, but also to make his first successful singing invasion of Europe.

As a boy, Harry had fallen on a pair of shears and injured his eye. During his years as a performer, nervous tension had weakened the membranes of his eye. When Belafonte was working on a TV show, it is reported that a piece of scenery accidentally fell and hit him. Although it was a serious blow, Belafonte paid no attention to it once the initial shock wore off.

The show, which was the cause of what was to appear later as major eye damage, had been important to Belafonte at this time because it was a black show. Nat (King) Cole had a regular show on TV, the only one on TV that starred and was titled after a black artist. In 1957, Cole was to TV what Jackie Robinson had been to baseball.

Unfortunately, because they were unable to get advertisers to support the show, in spite of high audience ratings, the show was not doing well. Belafonte and others, both black and white, pitched in to try and help the show. Even though Belafonte and others appeared on the show, the network could not find a national sponsor because of the fear of antagonizing Southern markets.

After appearing on the unfortunate show, seemingly having no problems with his eye, Belafonte continued with his engagements. It seems that the blow from the falling scenery, however, had caused a detachment of the retina, a condition which makes images blurred or off focus. Harry began noticing that his right eye had, more and more, areas of blackness. He was to open in Washington, D.C., but he became concerned and went to see an eye specialist. The doctor said Harry had to go to a hospital immediately or face the possibility of losing sight in that eye.

Harry entered New York Hospital on August 21. He was made to lie completely still for eight hours in the same position. They needed to let gravity settle the elements in his eye which were floating. Then the doctors had him lie in another position for eight hours. Before he was through with this phase of his treatment, Belafonte had been forced to remain still for 32 hours. Given the fact that Belafonte was a man who was always on the move, this must have been extremely difficult.

The next part of the treatment was an operation, the

From Surgery to Stardom

first of three which would be required before the condition was corrected. Three days after he was admitted to the hospital Belafonte underwent a four-hour operation. Although the surgery went off without incident, it would be two weeks before the results were known. During those two weeks Harry had to wear bandages on both eyes and remain perfectly still. If he were to move, then the detachment might happen again and all the surgeon's work would be useless. It must have been a very depressing and anxious period for Belafonte. Fortunately, when the bandages were removed he was able to see out of the bad eye.

All seemed to be going well at this time. He went home with Julie, only having to wear glasses for a while. He did not like to appear in public with them, however, as they were not flattering. Harry and Julie lived in the Seventies off Central Park West, the same place where Belafonte had lived when he first set up bachelor quarters. It was said that even though Belafonte was making nearly one million dollars a year, he still lived in a place where he had to walk to the cellar and empty his own garbage. It seemed that no matter how famous Belafonte might be, when he went to rent an apartment, landlords saw him as black.

Still, the apartment must have seemed like a palace after Belafonte's stay in the hospital. The stay in the hospital, with eyes completely bandaged, must have been a time of great fear for the performer. Harry at home could eat Julie's West Indian dishes, which she had learned to make. However, he was only home a few days when the vision in his right eye became clouded again.

Harry, trying to pretend that it was only temporary,

became depressed and fearful. Finally his wife suggested they call the doctor. Upon examination of the eye, the doctor said that the eye was healing, but there might be a recurrence of the retina detachment. He needed to check into the hospital again to rest and to have some tests.

The following day he underwent a second operation to correct a partial recurrence of the retinal detachment. The operation was successful, the detachment was corrected. Harry did, though, have to wear bandages for twenty-eight days. The muscles of the eye had been cut into twice, and they needed time to heal.

When Belafonte had been home from the hospital for nine days after the second operation, Julie went into labor with their child. On September 24, 1957 she gave birth to David Michael Belafonte.

The only problem at this time was that the second surgery had created another problem. One of the eye muscles had probably been cut too long or too short, causing the right eye to go slightly off-center. In an attempt to avoid another operation, Harry was given special glasses, designed to center the eyeballs. Of course the "matinee idol" could not be seen in public, nor could he perform in the glasses. Thus he wore them only in private.

During a Christmas party, one of Belafonte's friends observed that when Harry took off his glasses one of his eyes was off to the side. The adonis, the sex-symbol, looked like a sad little boy who was cross-eyed. It was indeed a sad sight.

It soon became evident to Belafonte that he could make no public appearances while he was wearing the glasses. Also, the sedation he had been given in order to keep him cool and calm while the glasses corrected his eyes made it difficult for him to make recordings and do performances. When he attempted to record his new album, *Belafonte Sings the Blues*, it didn't have any zest. Harry was on tranquilizers because of his condition, and the recordings didn't turn out right. So they sent the musicians home and postponed the recording session.

Belafonte had not been able to make public appearances during the months since his surgery. He'd spent his time planning the films he wanted to produce through his own company, Harbel. For an active man like Belafonte, waiting for the healing must have been difficult. Upon visiting his doctor that February, the results were not good. The eye was still off-center and the doctor felt another operation was necessary.

After seeing another specialist in Boston, at the doctor's request, Belafonte checked into the hospital once more. The Boston doctor had recommended a new approach to the surgery. The problem was that in attempting to correct the off-centeredness, the retina might again be detached. However, taking the Boston doctor's suggestion of tackling one eye through the other, the doctor completed Harry's third surgery. Everything was successful this time. The eye returned to the center. Belafonte, after five traumatic months, was fully recovered and ready to work again.

In March, Harry returned to the recording studio and cut his blues album. This time the recording date was successful; Harry sang with conviction and fervor. Only two cuts were recorded at this time, as Belafonte was shooting his first independent film in New York. He also had an engagement at the Greek in Hollywood to fulfill. In June of 1958, the blues album was completed.

It is thought that Belafonte never recorded a blues album before in his successful career because he felt maturity was necessary in order to sing the music of his own people. If jazz is the creation of the black in the instrumental field, then blues are the Negro's unique contribution to the vocal field. Harry felt that blues and spirituals were the most influential, the strongest songs in the American tradition, at least in terms of lyric content. He identified strongly with blues.

Also, Belafonte could sing the blues and just be himself, sing what he felt. When he started as a professional singer, he had been involved in the modern trends of jazz. When singing the kind of jazz that was popular in the early Fifties, he had been forced to adhere to the structure. It was hard to sing the way he felt to that type of music. Now, in 1958, Belafonte had his own set of values; he could sing the blues and emote what he felt in the music.

At various times Belafonte has mentioned the blues singers who have influenced him. He admired Mahalia Jackson and Billie Holiday, as well as Memphis Slim and Big Bill Broonzy. These blues singers went back to the beginnings of their music; they were basic, relating to their environment and knowing who they were. The blues of those singers was not contrived or mannered.

Belafonte was also influenced by Leadbelly and Odetta. Leadbelly was the blues singer with the twelve-string guitar who was twice convicted of murder. He also was twice released because of his music. Leadbelly made the hit, "Goodnight, Irene." It was people like Leadbelly and Mahalia Jackson, the great gospel singer, who impressed on Belafonte the massive amount of material that still exists in black culture and life. Many of these songs have yet to be found and interpreted. Such performers have also given Belafonte pride in blues material, the material of the black culture, and thus pride in himself.

Odetta had much influence on the blues singing of Belafonte also. Belafonte was so impressed with the singing of this Alabama woman that he introduced her to a nationwide audience on a CBS television spectacular which was aired December 10, 1959. Odetta was a large woman with operatic training. She recorded several albums, and appeared at the 1959 Newport Folk Festival and such places as the Hungry I in San Francisco and the Gate of Horn in Chicago.

Harry was indebted to Odetta because in her blues songs she expressed the inner meaning of the songs, transforming a melody into a dramatic experience. Her dramatic interpretation of songs aided Harry in approaching his songs with a sharper sense of their meaning, a searching concentration on their lyrical content.

Odetta, who was trained in opera, devoted herself to spirituals, blues and folk songs after 1953. Harry was so impressed by her singing that, not only did he present her on his TV spectacular, but he also annotated one of her LPs, *My Eyes Have Seen*. Odetta is described as having the range of a young Leadbelly at times, and then being able to switch to a rich, deep quality like that of Marian Anderson. Belafonte admired Odetta's strength, her simplicity and her humanity as it was expressed in her songs. The defiant strength of the black singer when singing his or her own basic inherited material is also noticeable in such singers as Leadbelly and Mahalia Jackson.

If Belafonte admired such blues singers as Odetta and Leadbelly for their strength and simplicity, it was also a blues singer's dramatic interpretation of a work which made him or her outstanding. The interpretation of a song could, of course, only be excellent if the song itself had meaning. Belafonte had always been known as a singer who refused to do tunes if the lyrics weren't meaningful. This was one of the reasons he left the pop-jazz field. He considered the songs which were being sung in these genres lacking in meaning. Harry was known for wanting his songs to express growth on his part, to provide some new insight that he could feel and thus move the listener.

If the blues are the black's contribution to vocal music, it is perhaps because they represent the feelings of blacks from far back. Just as the natives of Trinidad used calypso to express among themselves what they were thinking, what they knew, so the blues is the history and the thoughts of blacks in America. The blues started from the bottom, where people had wants and hopes. A part of a black man's needs were satisfied if he could sing the blues.

It is said that the blues are a test among black jazz musicians of their ability with music. Thus, at a time when Harry was receiving criticism from blacks about his marriage to a white, and his involvement with blacks was being challenged, it was only natural that he would sing the blues. The blues is a statement of identification with black heritage.

From Surgery to Stardom

Unfortunately, although psychologically and musically the importance of Harry's blues album cannot be denied, the content and the monotony of mood in the album kept it from being a big seller. Harry chose recent blues songs rather than going back to some of the great old traditional ones. Five of the songs were found in a Ray Charles album. The other six songs were contemporary.

Perhaps one reason Belafonte chose songs already recorded by Charles was that he had great admiration for the work of Ray. Charles, from the South, was only in his twenties at this time. Blind since the age of six, Ray Charles had learned music in a school for the blind. His music combined gospel with blues and modern jazz. He became accepted by the rock and roll set as well as the Newport Jazz crowd. He had won the Grand Prix of the French Academy of Recorded Music.

Of course, Harry's interpretations of Ray's songs were his own. They don't resemble one another in tone or mood. Charles' style comes from a country-gospel tradition, and Harry's from an urban-theatrical background. It is said that in the records, Charles is self-possessed and defiant while Harry is analytical and self-pitying. If Charles affirms, then Belafonte is introspective. One author has also pointed out that the contrast in the two men's singing represents the contrast between folk blues and modern blues. Ray Charles represents the old "shout" style of Bessie Smith, Ma Rainey and Leadbelly. Harry's rendition of the blues is more polished, smoother, in the tradition of Billie Holiday or Ella Fitzgerald. If the blues started in the South, people like Belafonte urbanized them.

The blues album was not extremely successful. The

moods of self-pity, the softness and slow tempo are monotonous, something one rarely finds in Belafonte. There is not the usual Belafonte dramatic tension and excitement in this album. Perhaps Harry's album would have done better had he selected material from folk-blues. Perhaps he would have fared better with his own people had he chosen older standards. However, the album was extremely important in the evolution of Belafonte as a person and an artist. Harry felt that Ray Charles knew how to savor and take advantage of his folk heritage in order to mold his own identity. What Charles did was to write and sing songs which came directly out of a people's traditions and needs. Also, for Harry, even though his album did not achieve great success, it was important in that it was a statement of his identity. In making a statement of his identity, he was making a statement of his maturity. He knew who he was.

Besides recording a blues album in 1958, after his three eye operations, Belafonte also invaded Europe and found incredible acceptance in the same year. In the summer of 1958, Harry, Julie and their young son David set out for Europe. He was to play at the Brussels World's Fair as well as in England, Paris, Berlin, Frankfort, Munich, the Scandinavian countries and Rome.

In England his concert at the Goumont State Theater was a sell-out. England was especially appreciative of Belafonte because of his record, "Mary's Boy Child," which had sold over a million copies in the British Isles. This is really a big success, if one remembers that England only has one-third the population of the U.S.

Not only were his eight concerts in England a sellout in advance, but the audiences did not want the performer to leave the stage, even though his concert ran 120 minutes. Although Belafonte was not singing new tunes at the Gaumont performances, he constantly practiced with his group of musicians, perfecting his numbers.

In Paris, playing at the Palais de Challot, Harry was also a great success. The booking agent had booked him at this smaller place, seating only 200, because he hadn't been sure how Belafonte would be received. Harry had never played in Paris, and some American performers were not selling. Also, he wasn't sure how Parisians would take to a folk, spiritual, calypso repertoire.

Harry's program was arranged in three parts: "Moods of the American Negro," "Songs of the Caribbean," and "Around the World." He was a sensation. The Parisian reviewers were very enthusiastic about Belafonte. By the time Harry had completed his four-day concert stay in Paris, the man who had booked him in the smaller theater knew that Harry could have packed the place for a month.

Even though Belafonte sang in many countries where people couldn't possibly understand his language, he felt that he had "communicated" in a very special way with Europeans. He could see that world art forms were becoming more and more related, because European audiences were just as enthusiastic about his music as American ones.

Thus the triumphant Belafonte returned to New York, only to find that his status remained the same—he might be an international star, but he was still black.

BELAFONTE

The Belafonte's wanted an apartment on Manhattan's East Side in midtown New York City. However, they could not find one. The story goes that when the newspapers printed this information, Mrs. Franklin Delano Roosevelt offered to buy a building with Belafonte.

However, Belafonte was not looking for a simple solution to racial prejudice. He instead moved into a ten-room apartment which was offered to him on the West Side, considered to be less desirable than the East Side.

His way to fight for civil rights was to join in some of the protest movements. Two weeks after his return from Europe, Belafonte participated in a demonstration for Negro rights in Washington, D.C. He and other such prominent people as Mrs. Martin Luther King and Jackie Robinson led a march of several hundred black and white students down Constitution Avenue to the Lincoln Memorial. After that procession, Belafonte was a spokesman for a group of twelve who went to the White House to present a petition. No one would let them into the grounds, supposedly because they did not have an appointment with the President.

Along with his problems as a black, Belafonte was also an outstanding success as an entertainer. On Thanksgiving in 1958, Belafonte appeared at the Waldorf in New York. The overflowing house was extremely enthusiastic, begging him to do one encore after another. The turnaways were becoming so great during this performance that the Waldorf moved Belafonte into the Grand Ball Room which seated 1,200 diners. It was the first time in the Waldorf's history that it had been forced to close the smaller Empire Room because of a flood of reservations.

Harry made a TV appearance on November 9th of that year. Inevitably there were racial problems. It is reported that a negro-hater in Alabama had knocked the station off the air by placing a chain across a power cable at the station's transmitter. Belafonte, who had turned down an Ed Sullivan offer earlier because the short periods allotted to performers was so limiting, accepted the Steve Allen show where he was allowed to perform for twenty minutes. This would let him change his pace, something he considered important to a successful performance. Also, he was allowed to produce the segment himself without interference. The appearance included folk ballads, spirituals and calypso.

If Belafonte was reluctant about appearing on American TV, he was pleased when the British asked him to do some performances on English television. One reason the offer from the British Isles was pleasant was that the English did not have commercials. This meant that Belafonte could sing and say things more openly, not dependent on sponsor approval. In the States, sponsors were unwilling to do anything that might hurt sales in the South.

While Belafonte had been playing London, he had not been allowed to appear on TV for fear that this would lessen box office sales. When his concert stay was over, he gave a one-hour program on the BBC. It was said that this concert got the highest rating of any previous broadcast on the BBC, except for the Coronation. When Harry returned to the States, the BBC sent an agent to negotiate a five-year deal with him. The papers were signed by Christmas, and it is reported that the BBC had given Belafonte the highest individual fee in its history. Reports were that the fee was somewhere around $70,000. Belafonte was to make seven appearances on the BBC.

Belafonte was of course asked why he had accepted the BBC offer while he had rejected TV series offers for huge sums of money on American TV. Harry felt that in England there were no Southern markets to keep him from performing artistically as he felt he should. In the States it seemed that he could not do what he wanted on TV. There would not be people between him and the audience he wanted to reach in England. In the States there always was the danger of panic on the basis of what a sponsor thought or what the rating reports would show. In England, the BBC gave Belafonte a sense of greater freedom than he felt on American TV. As an artist and as a person he wanted authority to determine the content of his own show. The BBC of course had rules too; they didn't want anything immoral or unpleasant. However, they did not have the problem of deciding whether the sponsor would approve of such and such an act or song. Their censorship was fair.

The British expected Belafonte's "Mary's Boy Child" to be as big a seller in Christmas of 1958 as it had been in 1957. It had sold by 1958 the fastest million copies in the history of the English record business. Some were saying that this song would become as big a classic as Bing Crosby's "White Christmas." Belafonte recorded the song in 1956. The calypso Christmas tune had seemed to be public domain. Unfortunately it was found that it had been copyrighted before Harry and Lord Burgess had done their version. Thus Belafonte, on his version, had to give credit to the first writer.

Regardless who got credit for writing the song first, a British newspaper commented that based on sales figures it seemed that everyone in England with a record player had a copy of "Mary's Boy Child" sung by Belafonte.

Belafonte was asked a lot of questions while he was in Europe about the integration problems in America and about his opinions on racial matters. The question of Little Rock came up. This was the time when the Supreme Court had ordered the integration of Little Rock schools. There had been a lot of racial trouble after this decision had been handed down. Harry, as an artist and as a black, felt obliged to give opinions to the Europeans on this and other racial matters; it was a responsibility. The problem in Little Rock was horrible. Yet, it was wonderful in a way, a sure sign of progress. The first sign of progress was that the Supreme Court had handed down such a decision. The trouble in Little Rock, the resistance, was the conflict which would result in change. You can't have change without conflict sometimes. Many felt that it would have been grand if integration could have taken place without troops. However, the fact that it was taking place, troops or no troops, was a sign of progress.

At the close of 1958, Belafonte had been both triumphant in Europe and of service to his people both in Europe and the United States. He also, after a frightening few months, had his eyesight restored.

Chapter Ten
The Moviemaker

Belafonte, having acted in many films, was interested in independent movie making. After his domestic situation had cleared up in 1957, he formed Harbel Productions, a name made from the first two syllables of his own name. Actually, Harry did not make any films until April, 1958, after his eye operations had been completed.

Harry did not think of himself as a spokesman for his race. However, just as Jackie Robinson had only wanted to play baseball, but ended up being a symbol in the eyes of the nation, Harry knew he too had become a symbol. Yet, the real reason for forming his own film company was to be able to do films he considered worthwhile, films the movie industry was not doing. Just as Belafonte wanted to sing songs with meaningful lyrics, so he wanted to be involved in films which were meaningful to him.

The first production of Harbel was to be a film called *The Brothers,* written by a black writer. Then, Harry wanted to do a film based on a prophetic novel, *The Purple Cloud.* This film, done with MGM, was to be called *The End of the World.* Then there was another shift in plans. After his second eye operation, Harry decided that, in a distribution tie-up with United Artists, he would do a film version of his own nightclub act. Harry also wanted to do a film biography of Martin Luther King. At that time, 1957, King was known as a courageous black minister who became nationally known when he led the Negro boycott of Alabama buses. Not too much later a berserk woman in Harlem had stabbed him. It was said that Belafonte had received money from United Artists for the research and writing of this film.

At the end of 1957, Harry started production on his original idea, *The End of the World.* The title was later changed to *The World, The Flesh and The Devil.* This film, although it was not considered great by the critics—mainly because of the ending and the way the racial message was handled—was significant to Harry's career. The film was considered good, and his acting was considered to be very good. Also, in his choice of subject for his first independent film, he indicated a mature, serious entry into the world of film production. It became obvious upon production of this film that Harry was seriously using the film medium to contribute insight to the racial problem. His position as a black would be central to his planning of future movies.

The Moviemaker

The film starred Harry, Mel Ferrer and Inger Stevens. They are the three sole survivors on earth. The film, although it is eerily set in an empty New York City, is not really a science fiction movie. Rather it is interested in the social frictions which are present even among the last three people on earth. Two are white and one is black. The twilight of the earth is portrayed in a haunting, provocative way in this drama. The story, directed by Ranald MacDougall, has an unnamed power begin an invasion with atomic radiation dust that soon engulfs and desolates the world.

Belafonte is a coal miner from Pennsylvania who got trapped in a sealed shaft. Since the shaft saved his life, he is able to emerge, only to find himself apparently alone. Having worked his way to freedom after several days, he is amazed that there are no people on the streets. He walks, runs and acts in a bewildered manner, like an animal. He can see all around him the vestiges of flight and panic.

Gradually he realizes that he is the only one left. He settles down in a fancy apartment. He can have any of the material things of life at will, but there are no people. He starts talking to a pair of manikins.

Critics praised Belafonte's acting in this first part of the film, in which he is the only actor. He is alone and feeling first confusion, then panic and fear, and also a terrible loneliness. Harry's ability to emotionalize in a setting was considered superb. There is one scene where he was told to go into a wrecked church, to sit in a pew, and to cry. It is said that during filming, Harry was able to spontaneously break into tears and sobs, lending reality to the scene.

After the first minutes of the film, Belafonte meets another survivor, a woman. As he is wandering around the completely deserted streets of New York City, he finds a woman who escaped the bomb because she was in a decompression chamber. Even though the two care for each other, there is the problem that they are of different races. Even though they seem to be the only two people left, the question of intermarriage becomes an issue.

The racial issue is treated in much the same way as it was in *Island In The Sun*. There, Harry told Joan Fontaine that their marriage wouldn't work out, that some day she might remind him that he was black. Here, the couple in *The World* is kept apart by Harry's fears that latent prejudice may rise to the surface and ruin their relationship. To complicate things even more, a third survivor appears, a white male. Now the issue of mixed marriage becomes instead a complicated, interracial love-triangle.

The movie is developed as a suspenseful melodrama. There is no easy solution to the problems of racial discrimination. What happens in the film is that the three people reach an understanding that, in order to survive, they must work together. However, they do nothing to resolve the love triangle. Philosophically the film is supposed to point out that man must work together to overcome his inhumanity toward other men, or the world will become very lonely and very tragic.

If the three did agree to work together, they could not agree what to do about love. At the end of the film, the white man and the black man have somehow settled their differences and the three of them are seen walking hand in hand down an empty Rector Street. As the three survivors walk off, the words that are seen over them, which grow in size on the screen, are not "The End." There is instead a large, flashing "The Beginning," indicating that their decision to be friends is at least a start.

There have been comments as to how the film might have ended in a more satisfying way, giving some resolution to the love-triangle. Perhaps if the girl had chosen the white man, she would have favored the segregationists and white supremists. She could have chosen the black man, but that would have opened the film to boycotts and hurt its bookings. There could have been an indication that she had chosen to love both of them, thus perpetuating the races. The ending, no matter how it was treated, would have been difficult. They could have indicated that the three were going to lead sexless lives, thus producing no more people. As the film did end, the girl chose neither man; thus the moviegoer was left with a generalized concept that all people need to work together, whether they be black, white, male or female.

Although the notices on *The World, The Flesh and The Devil* were not great, mainly because of the handling of the race question, the comments on Belafonte's acting were very positive. He had not gotten such good notices for his acting job in *Island In The Sun*. He had been accused of being static and not very convincing. Nevertheless, in *The World* he was called versatile and persuasive. One reviewer commented on the pacing he gave to the film by his subtle play of moods. It was said that the personal magnetism which is so effective in

Harry's nightclub act was not appearing on the screen.

The film's camera work, the eerie scenes of an empty New York City, as well as the script, direction and musical score were considered good by most critics. There was, though, much criticism of the treatment of the racial issue in the film. *Playboy* felt that the movie was "over-preachy." Another magazine felt that the film evaded the issue it raised. It was not made clear what was going to happen to the trio. Were they to be polygamous or sexless? Since no answer was given, it was assumed by one critic that the racial issue had only been put into the story as a gimmick, not as an important matter. This last comment is interesting as the racial issue had been so important to Belafonte.

Not only was there a racial issue in the film like that of *Island In The Sun,* that of a black-white relationship, but there was also the practical problem in the film, just as there had been in *Island*—should the black man and white woman kiss? In *The World* it was decided that there was no need for the couple to kiss. There is a scene where Harry cuts Inger Stevens' hair, and he touches her chin in one scene, and at the end he holds her hand, but there is no kissing scene.

There were problems with the racial element in the film, even though there were no kissing scenes. One story tells of a drive-in movie theater in Alabama where the picture was ordered stopped by the sheriff's office. It seems that this drive-in was segregated—blacks on one side and whites on the other. The whites were said to have been complaining about the conduct of the blacks. There were other incidents, in the North as well as the South.

However, at the time of the release of the film, 1959,

The Moviemaker

Harry and many other people in show business were doing all they could to help the race problem. Steps were definitely being made. That movies with interracial themes were being shown to the American public was progress in itself.

Harry was very serious about using the film medium to give insight into the racial problem. The fact that the end of *The World* was not a satisfactory racial statement to most does not take away from the seriousness of Belafonte's intent. It seemed that Belafonte's position as a black was very important to his thinking concerning his film productions.

However, Belafonte made a distinction; he could make films using blacks as actors and as subject matter, but they didn't all have to deal with racial conflict. He could also go outside the States to find subjects. He wanted to find areas in which blacks as artists could perform and function. At the time of the release of *The World,* Hollywood producers had trouble deciding to do films about blacks unless there was a theme of conflict. Now we have TV programs about blacks and movies about blacks where the issues are not the struggle for integration or some such matter. However, in 1959, these ideas were new. Harry spoke of doing a film on Pushkin. The story would have nothing to do with the fact that Pushkin was black.

At about this time, Belafonte and Sidney Poitier were able to discuss the problems of the black performer and the need for integrated story lines in films on national TV. The show was David Susskind's *Open End*. The two black professionals talked about the problems of the black performer. The black performer was responsible to his audience generally, but also specifically to the people of his race. Hopefully, the time would come when a man could be an artist first. At this time, a black could not be just a human being caught up in a conflict. He was first of all a black man.

In order to try and promote black actors in roles just as people, Actors Equity put on a show which was titled "The Integrated Showcase." An attempt was made to show that blacks could be cast in white acting roles without changing what the author was trying to say. Most of the comments on this showcase were that the time was not yet right, that the audience couldn't forget that an actor on the stage was black. Thus, using a black in a part that was not intended specifically as a black role would distort the production.

Variety wrote that it was unfortunate racial consciousness was still so backward. It stated that integration was still a social issue, with powerful emotional overtones. The average theatergoer was not ready to accept a black in a white role. *Variety* felt that possibly mixed cast shows like "The Integrated Showcase" might hasten the day of integrated casting. In 1959 there were even some mixed cast productions. There was one production, *The Winner,* in which a black was used as a judge who presided over the divorce case of a white couple. Also, in the musical *Jamaica,* Lena Horne and Ricardo Montalban played very romantic love scenes together. Today we accept a black in *Ironside* along with other police who happen to be white. Also, there was *The Rookies,* where one of the rookie cops was black.

It is due to blacks like Belafonte and Poitier that the plight of the Negro in the entertainment profession has become better. Belafonte and Poitier will go on to make films together. In these movies they will both be very conscious of the role of the black in the story.

In *The World, The Flesh and The Devil,* Belafonte sang a song, "Fifteen," which was a love ballad. It is said that in spite of the liveliness of some of the calypso songs, the boisterousness of some of the folk ballads, a majority of his songs are gentle love ballads. This is said to reflect the true character of Belafonte. Under all the early hostility, the hilarious singer of wild folk songs and the hard driving professional, is a core of sensitivity and fragility. The song "Fifteen" was recorded in an album, *Love Is A Gentle Thing,* in 1958.

In Belafonte's next film, *Odds Against Tomorrow,* he was both the star and a fully independent United Artists producer. He had only been co-producer of *The World, The Flesh and The Devil. Odds Against Tomorrow* was to be the first of six films that Belafonte planned to star in and produce for United Artists.

Odds was taken from a book by William P. McGivern. In the film, the message seemed to be that racial hatred leads to disaster. Yet, in the book, because the characters develop differently, the story has a different slant. In the book, Earl Slater (Robert Ryan) is a Negro-hater. Before the end of the story he will develop and regenerate. Earl Slater finds his prejudices gradually dissipated, in spite of himself, because the black, played by Belafonte, makes sacrifices for him.

At the end of the book, although Slater's selfish girl friend (Shelly Winters) talks him into deserting his black accomplice, he changes his mind and returns to help the black man. As they are bank robbers, Slater is killed and the black man is captured alive. The sheriff admires Slater's change of heart which cost him his life, but he doesn't quite understand the man's reason for such a sacrifice.

In the movie version of *Odds Against Tomorrow*, Earl Slater is a static character. He begins as a man who is full of hate and is ultimately destroyed by that hate. The black, Belafonte, also does not change his character in the film. There is not only tension around the bank robbery that is being planned, but also around the potentially explosive situation between Slater and the black man. The black man is totally hostile, just as is Slater.

One critic wrote that the mood, atmosphere and characterization were well developed in the film, that the movie was a superior holdup drama. Director Robert Wise was given praise for his work. The film was shot in New York, and was considered to be dramatically forceful by one critic. The story is of the plan for a holdup of an upstate bank by three desperate men. The preparation and committing of the robbery was presented with a building tension, leading to a shattering climax. As the story progresses the characters of the people are outlined and their personal problems delineated. Of course, a major part of the story revolves around the clash and conflict between the white man and the black.

Ryan is portrayed as a hard, prejudice-ridden character who lives with Shelley Winters. Belafonte is a gambling nightclub entertainer who owes an underworld loan shark a sum of money and has to meet the debt or risk his life. Ed Begley plays a vengeful ex-cop who masterminds the bank holdup. The cast includes Gloria

Grahame, a girl next door who makes a seductive approach to Ryan; Will Kuluva, an underworld figure; and Kim Hamilton, playing the ex-wife of Belafonte.

The robbery is to be in Melton, New York. There are all kinds of character clashes and expressions of ambitions en route to the holdup. The end of the film is death for both men. As both are proud, and as they both will not give, they end up having to shoot it out. In the film version there is an implied message that we face long odds against tomorrow coming at all unless we develop some understanding and tolerance today.

If the book tended to deal quite a bit with the change in character of Earl Slater, then the film fully explores the experiences and motivations of the black as played by Belafonte. His loving relationship with his daughter is portrayed. Also his frustrated dealings with his estranged wife, whose white friends are unpleasant to him, is portrayed in the film. Even though the study of the character of the black man gives dimension to the film, the film loses something by not dealing with the change in character in Slater. In having him remain mean, the film instead emphasizes the destructive consequences of Slater's feelings, whereas the book presented a different reason for Slater's death.

Perhaps the book was also more thrilling, as the tension before and after the robbery was demonstrated. In the film, one critic said the movie lost momentum at the end because it was not clear whether it was supposed to be a crime movie or a message film.

Harry's role becomes interesting, though, because of the shift in plot emphasis and direction. As a youth Harry was hostile; he plays a hostile, proud, defiant, unyielding black man in the film. If he had little to be hostile about in 1959, he still had philosophical and social reasons to portray the injustices toward the black in his society. In *Odds* he presents an integrated PTA meeting, perhaps as a message. Also, the angry character of the black hero is a statement of racial concern.

The criticisms of Belafonte's performance in *Odds Against Tomorrow* were very positive. The feelings about the film itself were mixed. One reviewer said that the film was very sharp from the point of production and that it was dramatically explosive. Another critic wrote that the film was almost too angry.

One reviewer priased the photography and the naturalness of the dialogue. The message of racial hatred leading to chaos was said to have been done unobtrusively. This was a welcome critique in the light of the fact that Belafonte's previous film, *The World, The Flesh and The Devil,* had been called "over-preachy." The direction of the film was said to be sensitive, having paid attention to psychology and characterization. *Variety* wrote that it was a good picture and good box office.

The criticisms about the excess of hostility were in line with Belafonte's desire to ultimately do films which did not involve the black man in conflict with his environment. It is said that Belafonte looked forward to the day when he would do a Cary Grant type of film. He would later be involved in a comedy with Poitier, and also a non-racial film with Zero Mostel. However, at this point in his career, the particular subjects found in *Odds* and *The World, The Flesh and The Devil* were what he decided to produce.

The critics agreed that Belafonte's acting in *Odds* was very good. He gave a good performance, they felt, and the scenes with his wife and daughter were very moving. *Variety* said it was the most sustained acting job Harry had done to date. Another critic wrote that Belafonte had now achieved dramatic maturity, that he was commanding and imaginative as an actor.

When one realizes that this last praise of Belafonte's maturity as an actor came about ten years after Harry had unsuccessfully tried to get acting work, the full importance of the statement can be appreciated. He had tried unsuccessfully to get acting work in the late Forties, and had finally turned to singing as an alternative to working in the garment center. Now, having achieved stardom as a singer, he was starring in and producing his own films. He was also getting good reviews.

If Belafonte had matured as an actor after ten years as a performer, his friends and acqaintances saw a maturity in him as a person also. Where he had once been tense and hostile, he had become more relaxed. When he spoke of plans for the future they were confident, rational plans. His restlessness and impatience was now being channeled into enterprises. The anger and protest that he had exhibited as a beginning performer had turned into personal magnetism, humor, tenderness, sexuality, with only a touch of hostility.

Still, if Belafonte lost his hostility which came from feeling underprivileged because he was black, he did not lose his desire to help his race. He was conscious of the contribution he wanted to make in the fight for equal rights. His concern, instead of scribbling words on subway posters as he had done in the past, was now how to use the screen medium most effectively to work for equal rights.

His concern for blacks and their heritage, as well as an interest in helping the black artist, was apparent. His independent movie productions in the late Fifties gave insight into the character of blacks and their inolvement with whites. He presented Odetta to the public in a TV spectacular, along with drawings by the black painter Charles White. He introduced the South African singer Miriam Makeba to The Village Vanguard.

Typical of the energetic Belafonte, at the same time he was involved in promoting his film *Odds Against Tomorrow,* he was involved in producing a Broadway play. However, if his film *Odds* was not turning out to be a big box office hit, this play did not turn out to be one either; it closed after three days.

Harry had become interested in *Moonbirds* while filming *Odds*. The play starred comedian Wally Cox and was a comedy written by the Frenchman, Marcel Ayme. The play had done well in France. It was the story of a young professor who was able to turn people into birds. He did this when he located people who were in trouble or in pain. However, the young professor, who was only trying to help people, got into trouble with the law.

Harry felt that it was too bad that works of merit were difficult to do on Broadway because of the high cost of production. Only things which could be commercially successful were done because of the high expense of production. This play, which had artistic merit, did not receive positive reviews. Nevertheless, Belafonte was perhaps realizing a dream in being a producer. He

The Moviemaker

who had not been able to get a job as an actor on Broadway was now in a position to produce Broadway productions.

The years of Belafonte's involvement in major dramatic productions were just beginning in 1959. *Ebony* magazine devoted time in several articles to Belafonte's ventures as an independent movie producer. In one article, dated June 5, 1959, the magazine explained that Belafonte was a good business man. It stated that as the laws stood in 1959, movie stars found it more profitable tax wise to produce their own pictures than to work for other companies.

Belafonte, by coming into the film business not only as a star but also as a producer, was following other top stars. He, in becoming a full, financing producer, was doing what has been done by John Wayne, Burt Lancaster, Kirk Douglas and Frank Sinatra. The production companies are formed for one reason, because they offer a tax advantage. Another reason why stars form their own companies is to have complete control over all aspects of the productions in which they appear.

Ebony wrote that *The World, The Flesh and The Devil* was a joint production of Harbel Productions and Sol C. Siegel Productions, Inc. The film cost $1,400,000 to put together. They quoted the Belafonte organization as contributing $250,000 to the film. Of the picture's gross profits, the Belafonte organization was to collect one-third.

For the next film, *Odds Against Tomorrow,* which cost $1,000,000 to produce, Belafonte's organization contributed $274,000 and United Artists the rest. Belafonte was allowed to control all hiring. He supervised the whole production and he appeared in the picture as one of the stars. He was to receive fifty percent of the film's gross profits.

Robert Ryan is said to have thought the movie would contribute to making democracy more complete. The film is an entertainment movie, but also a film making a social statement. Not only does the film star Robert Ryan and Belafonte, but also Ed Begley who plays the third bank robber. These three men, who execute the bank robbery, are not professional criminals, but each is involved in tragic and frustrating situations which makes them turn to crime. *Ebony* wrote that the end of the film was tragic, the central theme of the movie being the negative, corroding essence of hatred.

Ebony wrote of the racial aspects of Belafonte's creating his own production company, which gave him greater authority in the making of films. Belafonte wanted to make films which show blacks as they really are, not as white people see them. This same reason was perhaps why he turned down a role in *Porgy and Bess;* the blacks in that production were convicts, pushers, whores and cripples. Many blacks have reacted against the stereotyping of the black, the "Amos and Andy" treatment.

Ebony saw Belafonte as a great force who would affect the use and treatment of blacks by the film industry. Belafonte was said to be aware of the power of the n ovie medium as a means of altering social attitudes. His production company was a business venture but also a weapon against the stereotyping of blacks in films. The force of his company was socially constructive as he saw it. Both *The World, The Flesh and The*

The Moviemaker

Devil and *Odds Against Tomorrow* carry the same message—racial prejudice is harmful.

Belafonte was most conscious in 1959 of removing the stereotype of blacks from the entertainment field. He planned to make films showing blacks with the same hopes, problems, love as other people. He wanted to show blacks in his films who work, succeed, die, fall in love—everything that people in general do. He planned to have his blacks be those who make contributions to science, government and art.

In 1959, Harry planned to devote fifty percent of his time to making movies. Of course, his productions did not always turn out to be those he envisioned at a given time. However, the important thing was his scope and his energy. If he changed plans later and did a different story than expected, it was because after careful planning another story seemed the better idea.

In 1959 his plans were to do a western, *The Last Notch,* a story of the post-Civil War with a western setting. A western, *Buck and The Preacher,* done with Poitier, would appear in 1972. Then, there was the plan to do the life of Pushkin. Harry was to play the role of Pushkin, the great black Russian poet. It was reported that Belafonte had decided he wanted the talented Ingmar Bergman to direct this film. Bergman had been interested and he had been sent a round trip ticket to talk with Belafonte.

Whether or not all those plans reported in *Ebony* in 1959 came to be in their actual form is not important. Since 1959, Belafonte has achieved some excellent results in films, both as producer and actor. He has also, as *Ebony* and other magazines and newspapers reported, used his influence and his status as producer to help advance blacks in the movie industry.

Chapter Eleven
Harry the Man

Belafonte, after his first ten years in show business, was indeed successful. It is said that in the arts, the sign one is really successful, that one has arrived, is "the knock," the roast or the thorough, severe criticism. In 1959 Harry did get a written going over. The critic Maurice Zolotow wrote a scathing criticism of Belafonte on May 10, 1959. The piece appeared in the *American Weekly*.

There were some good things said about the entertainer in this article. Harry's unique donation to the folk ballad, his blending of the sex drive into it, was praised. He was also lauded for giving himself so much to his audience. Zolotow wrote that no matter how egocentric and perhaps selfish Harry might be, he had always participated with both time and money in charities, especially the NAACP. He also pointed out the strength Belafonte must have had to be able to overcome his personal and professional disasters. Harry, he said, did have a magic of personality and a great deal of courage.

However, the article was not concerned with just giving praise to the famous folk singer. Zolotow accused Belafonte of being the most egocentric of entertainers, of being pretentious, of thinking he was the first star of his race, of being basically unsure of himself, and of alternating between extreme highs and deep depressions. Zolotow also criticized him for not being a real folk singer. He chastised Belafonte for callously firing the manager who had helped him get started. More important, perhaps, Zolotow accused Harry Belafonte of wanting to be white. He criticized him for divorcing the black wife who supported him through his struggling years so that he could marry a white woman.

These were strong criticisms of Belafonte. One of Harry's friends suggested that perhaps Zolotow had written such a cruel expose of Belafonte because Harry had refused to permit him to write an article in Harry's name a couple of years before. The fact was brought up also by Belafonte's friends that Harry, not being pure black, having two white grandparents, could not completely identify with other blacks. Many people believe that as many as sixty-five percent of white Americans have black blood, and that because of slavery there are white genes in many blacks.

The accusation that Harry wanted to be white made Belafonte's friends angry. It was pointed out that Harry was very active in Youth Marches for Integration in

Harry the Man

Washington, and that he was always speaking on behalf of black causes. He was active in the NAACP. Also, it was pointed out in rebuttal to Zolotow's comment that if Harry wanted to be white, why did so much of his singing material come from black life and folklore from America and the West Indies?

Perhaps part of the price of fame was the criticisms Belafonte received from the press. A critic had also stated that Belafonte, though famous, only had a few real friends.

The comment that Harry wanted to be white had been attributed to his ex-wife Margurite, in spite of the fact that she explained the comment as meaning something quite different than the way it had been interpreted. It was not that Harry wanted to be white, but that he wanted to be accepted as white. She had been quoted in Zolotow's article as saying that Harry was so unhappy because he had never been able to accept the fact that he was black and always would be. However, the statement was said to be, not that Harry wanted to be white, but that he wanted to be accepted as a black man in a white world. Most blacks want to be accepted as blacks in a white world.

It has often been alleged that Harry shows this desire to be accepted in a white world by surrounding himself with whites. In 1959, it was said that his secretary was white, his publicity man was white, his conductor, his psychiatrist, and his managers and lawyers were white. The comment was made that when Belafonte was young he always complained about the lack of jobs for blacks; now he was not hiring them, at least in certain major capacities.

Belafonte also hired blacks. Perhaps by 1959 he felt accepted enough to be able to hire whoever he wanted for any position. The fact of the matter was that Belafonte, it seemed to some, just wanted to be able to move with ease in a white world. When he was young, he was angry at being excluded from a white world. He was excluded by whites in his neighborhood from social activities. He had not been allowed to stay in hotels where he was performing because he was black. Now, in spite of his fame and fortune, he could not live on New York's East Side. That was the reason he could not accept the every-day fact that he was black. Despite his popularity and success he was not welcome everywhere, he was not accepted by all whites.

The fact was also brought up that in 1959, while Belafonte did work to help the NAACP, he was not a member and he refused to join. As to his hiring of white employees, however, it was seen as an advantage by some of his friends. After all, a black person had to learn to get along in a white world. By learning to work with whites on a day-to-day basis, one is helping the cause of blacks. It's just as if you were trying to do business with people of a foreign country—if you speak the language of these people, you appeal to them. It was said that Belafonte should hire people because they were good at their job, not because they were white or black.

Another opinion at the time was that if a black and a white were both of equal competence, the black should be hired, as the opportunities for blacks were fewer. Although Belafonte did not make a statement about his employment policies, he did make it clear that he planned, through his movie production company, to employ black actors and talented blacks in other creative areas such as writing. At the time, he had a black executive in his film company and a black production stage manager. Later, during the filming of *The Angel Levine,* in the late Sixties, it will be shown how Belafonte worked to help blacks and other minorities get a foot into the film industry.

As for the criticisms of Belafonte's temper and the statement that he didn't have many friends, these things are hard to determine. The petty jealousies that must exist when a performer comes from the ghetto to become a superstar make it difficult to see who is a friend and who is just an acquaintance. Even in the case of Belafonte and Poitier, who were both successful, there were stories of feuds. As for the statements that Belafonte had a temper, there was certainly one example of it reported involving a performance at the Carter Barron Amphitheatre in Washington, D.C. It seemed Harry did not like the fact that a photographer was snapping pictures while he was performing. Later, he grabbed the man's camera and tore out the pictures. Supposedly, not only did Belafonte give the man $250 for any damage he might have caused, but he told him to feel free to take more pictures.

As for the comments that Belafonte was moody, depressed sometimes and elated at other times, this is not unusual for a person coming from so low in life and rising so high. The fact that he did undergo analysis indicated that he was working on difficulties stemming from the problem. That he was able to escape his background at all is amazing; that he was able to become a superstar, a black matinee idol and a hit in Europe was almost impossible. Anyone achieving such heights is bound to have some psychological problems.

Also, it is hard to assess how much Belafonte did or did not do for blacks. If he was or was not an actual member of the NAACP in 1959, it must be taken into consideration what he did for blacks because of his magnitude as a performer. He has been able to open doors that a less famous person would not have been able to open. There was an instance reported in 1955 in Las Vegas. In 1952, when playing in Las Vegas, Belafonte had been forced to stay in a segregated hotel, and was not allowed to use the hotel's facilities. In an account of a 1955 breakthrough, Arnold Shaw in this biography, *Belafonte, An Unauthorized Biography*, talks of how Belafonte, with the help of two friends, integrated a hotel swimming pool in Las Vegas.

It seems that by 1955, Harry was being allowed to stay at the hotel but couldn't use the pool or gamble in the casino. He got his friend Fran Scott to sit by the side of the "white" swimming pool. Then Harry and Tony Scott, dressed in bathing suits, dove into the pool. Several years before, at another hotel in Las Vegas, a well-known black performer had jumped into the pool. The management had drained the pool afterward. When the performer got into the pool again the next day, the management again drained the pool.

When Harry jumped into the water, the management didn't know what to do, they were so surprised. Then an interesting thing happened; white women started jumping in the pool to surround the handsome Belafonte. Then the kids jumped in. Pretty soon the mothers and fathers were asking Harry to pose with their children for pictures. One night Harry, having integrated the hotel's pool, integrated their gambling casino. People crowded around to watch him play. They also joined whatever game he played. The management decided that allowing Belafonte to use the casino was good for business.

There was another incident where Harry helped a female college and music student in Texas who was having trouble being allowed to perform in the University of Texas' musical productions. When she graduated and wanted to study voice in New York City, the Belafonte Foundation paid for her tuition as well as providing her a dance scholarship.

Belafonte, because of his fame, has had to endure racial snubs along with racial victories. It is said that when he was filming *Odds Against Tomorrow,* some pictures were taken of him with some female students from Vassar College. When the photographer forwarded the prints to the Vassar public relations office, he was surprised to find out that the school was angry, didn't want the photos used in print.

In spite of the scathing Zolotow article about Belafonte, he was as popular as ever at the close of his first ten years as a singer. *Time Magazine* published a four-page article on Belafonte on March 2, 1959, and it also placed him on the cover. The article was very complimentary, writing that Harry was at the peak of "one of the most remarkable careers in U.S. entertainment."

Time also pointed out that Harry had broken through a lot of color lines in the entertainment field—he'd been the first black to play certain posh nightclubs like the Eden Roc in Miami and the Palmer House in Chicago.

He also was a first with his romantic lead in the interracial film *Island In The Sun*. *Time* also stressed that Belafonte's charm had nothing to do with age, sex or color. One disc jockey said he could play a Belafonte record and not lose any part of the audience.

Time talked of how Belafonte had broken all attendance records when he toured Europe. It quotes Mrs. Eleanor Roosevelt as writing that Harry had an ability to mesmerize an audience, and it pointed out that not only was Belafonte extremely good-looking and very talented as a singer, but his nightclub acts were beautifully planned and executed.

As for Belafonte the man, *Time* had some interesting comments. It described Harry as moving in an interracial world, which, rather than being composed of blacks and whites, was primarily composed of show business people. Belafonte was quoted as saying that his son, David, would grow up in the same world in which he had lived. Harry didn't want to save his son from the feelings which go with such a heritage.

Time listed some of the causes to which Belafonte devoted himself in 1959. There was the NAACP and the Wiltwyck School for Boys. There was also the Rev. Martin Luther King's Montgomery Improvement Association. *Time* also reported that twenty percent of Belafonte's income went to the partly tax-exempt Belafonte Foundation of Music and Arts. This foundation had as a purpose to help young black people with talent to shake their bondage.

Time also wrote of Belafonte's legendary perfectionism, the fact that he worked over performances and recordings until they were perfect. It also wrote of Belafonte's good sense as a businessman and an entertainer. For example, in 1959, Harry was said to be going light for a while on the nightclub circuit, making instead some cross-country tours of college campuses and small-town auditoriums. He also felt that by getting in direct contact with college and small-town audiences he could revitalize his performance.

Belafonte also demonstrated keen business sense. He rarely appeared on TV so he would not be overexposed to the public. He also disliked TV appearances because the shortness of the segments on TV did not allow full development of a show. With records, he did not like to plug his own hits. He backed away from calypso, having already launched the craze, because it could limit him artistically. In 1958 he recorded a blues album, and in 1959 he recorded a romantic ballad album.

In closing, *Time* quoted Harry as having some concern for the longevity of his career, now into its second decade. However, *Time* did not feel the talented entertainer would have a problem.

Thus, for Zolotow's critical article about Belafonte, there were many complimentary ones by major magazines and papers. During 1959, the year in which these articles came out, Belafonte was not only involved in films. His nightclub schedule was full as usual.

In the summer of 1959 he packed the Greek Theater in Hollywood for three weeks, drawing $252,000. He filled the Red Rock Theater in Denver, a 12,500 seater, and he played to 6000 at the Forum in Vancouver. In all the places he broke attendance records. Reviews of his act were favorable. It seemed Belafonte was showing more growth as a performer. He had become more subtle, warmer and more emotional.

In August of the same year Belafonte took time out from his heavy schedule of concerts to appear on the NBC-TV panel program in Washington, "Youth Wants to Know." The mixed panel of students asked Harry about racial discrimination, about rock 'n' roll and other things. Belafonte had previously attacked rock 'n' roll, calling it musical rot. Belafonte was very frank in giving his opinions to the kids on the show.

One of the highlights of 1959 for Belafonte was his concert at Carnegie Hall in New York City. He gave two one-man concerts. They were both benefits, one for the Lincoln School, the school attended by his daughters, the other for the Wiltwyck School, which worked with emotionally disturbed boys. Mrs. Franklin Delano Roosevelt was a trustee for the latter school, to which Belafonte's performance was able to contribute $58,000.

The shows, on April 19 and 20, 1959, were highly successful. The critics wrote that Belafonte had achieved instant rapport with his audiences. He appeared in his traditional V-cut silk shirt and tight black pants. His act was divided into three parts; "Moods of the American Negro," "In the Caribbean," and "Around the World." He sang such black songs as "Sylvie," the Leadbelly favorite, "John Henry," and "When the Saints Go Marching In." Then he sang the favorite calypso ballads and songs. Some of the around the world tunes were the Israeli, "Hava Nagilah" and the songs of Haiti and Spain. The show concluded with the audience participating in "Matilda."

The first decade of Belafonte's career ended with

great success. In September, 1959, Belafonte was in London, appearing in his one-man BBC telecast. The future for the energetic Harry held many plans. He was planning to make a western with Sidney Poitier; he wanted to do a film on the life of Pushkin. He had many projects. The first ten years of his career had been good to him.

Chapter Twelve
Ten Powerful Years

As Harry's career rolled into its second decade, the entertainer continued to break box-office records all over the world. He also continued to make films, paying close attention to subjects which would be of help or of interest to his race. Belafonte also became known as a man who spoke out for what he believed.

In 1968, *Newsweek* covered a talk show Belafonte had hosted, telling of the serious, sometimes black-oriented subjects he had brought up during his week of hosting. The show was Johnny Carson's *Tonight Show*. Some of Harry's guests were his friends Bill Cosby, Sen. Robert Kennedy, Wilt Chamberlain, Zero Mostel, Marianne Moore, Sidney Poitier, Petula Clark, Paul Newman, the Smothers Brothers and Dr. Martin Luther King. To the millions of viewers, Belafonte was able to bring up some interesting matters on the usually light television show.

They discussed the government's neglect of blacks in Watts, the high suicide rate among unhappy American Indians. They also gave their opinions about President Johnson's handling of the Vietnam situation. It was reported by *Newsweek* that Senator Kennedy accused the cigarette industry of killing 350,000 Americans every year. The interesting fact is that one of the sponsors of the show hosted by Harry was a cigarette company. The Smothers Brothers had been told not to do certain jokes on their own show; however, Belafonte allowed them to do the jokes on the *Tonight Show*.

Even though Belafonte was an unusual host, not trying to get any laughs for himself, and bringing up very serious matters on the late-night fun show, his appearances topped the average ratings in New York for Johnny Carson himself. Belafonte did have some entertainment on his shows; Lena Horne sang and Bill Cosby did a number. *Newsweek,* titling the article "Belafonte Power," explained that even blacks like Bill Cosby and Sammy Davis Jr., when they had emceed the show, had not taken complete charge like Belafonte did. He personalized the show, having fifteen black guests out of the show's twenty-five. He and Sidney Poitier discussed a time when they were in Mississippi when the KKK chased them ten miles into the next county.

Belafonte was able to make his plea for integration, for acceptance of his race, in a non-preachy way. He showed home movies of his wife and his children watching him water ski in Las Vegas with a group of whites. By showing himself playing around in the water, having fun, he was able to make a statement about the need for acceptance of one another.

Newsweek wrote that the show exuded color consciousness. At one point, when Ed McMahon was doing a commercial about a product that would whiten and brighten the new miracle fabrics, Belafonte snapped jokingly, "Watch that stuff." The show was more seriously slanted than the usual Carson shows. Belafonte questioned Senator Kennedy about the possibility of his being a presidential candidate. Belafonte's strong opposition to the Vietnam situation was voiced more than once. Harry said, when Dr. King was on the show, that he strongly opposed the Vietnam war. He got Dr. King to talk about who he thought should get the 1968 protest vote. At the close of his week's stand-in as host for Johnny Carson, Belafonte had covered such serious matters as racial relations, politics and the current problems with Vietnam. The *Newsweek* review of the shows, stating the seriousness of the subjet matters, brings to mind earlier comments about Belafonte's relationship to his singing material and his films—he is very much concerned with content, and not interested in doing anything superficial and meaningless.

Belafonte's next film project turned out to be a social project also. Not only did he film *The Angel Levine,* but he gave several young blacks and Puerto Ricans the chance to get involved in the film industry. Belafonte, whose heavy nightclub schedule and other performance obligations had kept him from acting in films for several years, was with *The Angel Levine* to become involved in several films.

The Angel Levine, filmed in 1968, is listed as a fantasy melodrama. It was a United Artists release of a Belafonte Enterprises film, directed by Jan Kadar, who had directed *The Shop On Main Street*. The film, starring Belafonte and Zero Mostel, could have been uneven, since Mostel had such strong, forceful artistic presence and physical presence. However, Mostel was able to keep his performance within bonds so that Belafonte and the female lead, Ida Kaminski, held their own very well.

Belafonte played the part of the spirit of a petty thief. The fantasy was of contemporary nature; Zero Mostel was an old Orthodox Jewish husband on trial as a spirit. The old tailor, who was being buried by mounting difficulties, appealed to God for help. God sent an angel to help him. The angel was the spirit of a black street hustler, played by Belafonte. The tailor had to find someone in whom to believe, having asked God for help and thus having to show faith. Harry-the-hustler had to find a human being who believed in him. The hustler only had twenty-four hours to accomplish his mission. The film ended only quasi-successfully for the two of them. Belafonte did succeed in making the tailor believe in him, but it was after twenty-four hours. Neither of them got redemption.

Variety called the film touching, often sentimental. It called the film a "handsomely gritty Belafonte Enterprises production."

Another magazine discussed the relationship between this film and *Odds Against Tomorrow*. The article, entitled "Film is 'My Black Thing,' " appeared in *Ebony* in October of 1969. The magazine, describing the film *Odds,* wrote that the elaborate bank robbery plot, which ended in tragedy for the crooks because of their racial problems, proved by its lack of great success at the box office that the public was not quite ready for the type of social message portrayed in *Odds Against Tomorrow*. The film had demonstrated through the plot, perhaps, that crime only pays if there is racial harmony among the thieves. In this same magazine we found the comment that Belafonte felt that perhaps, ten years later, the public was ready for a social message.

The "Black Thing" Belafonte talked about was not only the content of the film this time; it was also his program set up around the film involving youths of minority classes. However, the film itself was created in the hopes that America had, in its movie and television industry, become more receptive to black people. The country had, hopefully, changed and advanced in the ten years which separated the two films.

The film contained people from very diverse backgrounds, thus promoting acceptance of people from all places. The director, Jan Kader, was Czechoslovakian. Ida Kaminski, the female lead, was Polish. Zero Mostel was an American Jew. The film also contained an Irishman from Ireland, Mila O'Shea. Gloria Foster, who played the thief's girlfriend, was a black woman from America. Since youths from black and Puerto Rican backgrounds were allowed to participate in the film's making, they were exposed to top talent from all over the world.

The parallel between the film and the incidents in the life of Martin Luther King were also unmistakable. There were twenty-four hours in which the United States could believe in Martin Luther King and his movement of non-violence. No one seemed to see the urgency of King's appeal. It seemed that in the twenty-fifth hour, when it was too late for King, blacks and whites were starting to believe in his mission. The question, as in the film, is, will there be another chance? Or is there only one chance?

The apprentices felt that they wanted to concern themselves with black films. This would not be the only area of concern. There had to be a period in which blacks were concerned with their blackness, just as Jews concern themselves with their jewishness. This race consciousness brings out frustrations and angers and is thus necessary therapy. Then one must face the world in general. Uniqueness as a black is important, but being a part of the human race is also important. Thus the youths being trained in the art of filmmaking would hopefully become involved in cinema as it relates to all people.

Ebony described the project in which Harry became involved with the filming of *Angel*. It stated that traditionally angels come to the aid of people in distress. Not only in this case did Harry, as an actor, come to the aid of an old Jewish tailor, but Belafonte the man acted as an angel in his efforts toward helping humanity. In the *Ebony* article, entitled "Belafonte Plays Angel On and Off Screen," the magazine described Belafonte's efforts to help young blacks learn movie-making techniques on the set of *The Angel Levine,* filmed in East Harlem in New York.

Fifteen young Puerto Ricans and blacks were, during the filming of *Angel,* given the chance to learn the art of making films. They worked alongside the talented Belafonte, Kadir, Mostel and the others. The film took three months to shoot. During this time the apprentices were paid $100 a week from a Ford Foundation grant of $25,000. The apprentices were aged from eighteen to thirty-four, and possessed a variety of experience in the film industry. They felt the experience had been valuable, even though because of union requirements they were not allowed to handle the cameras, sound or light equipment.

It is reported that even before the shooting of the film was over, some of the apprentices were already beginning to be offered jobs in the industry. The apprentices formed their own production company, Asone. This symbolized their spirit of unity. At the time of the publication of the *Ebony* article in 1969, the production company Asone had begun working on its first film, *The Cardboard Suitcase*.

The apprentices learned all the aspects of filmmaking. In the casting office they learned how to select actors and extras for certain parts. They learned how to determine the budget of a film. Other areas of behind-the-scene production learned by the apprentices were still photography and even script changes. The students worked directly with Zero Mostel and the director.

All areas of employment were envisioned by the apprentices. One girl wanted to be a script supervisor. Another student wanted to go into producing and directing. Because the program was a practical one, it dealt with practical issues. Not interested in training blacks to be just "movie stars," it wanted to help minorities get into all areas of film production. Belafonte felt that the black apprentices, remaining faithful to doing something about the black condition, would do themselves and their people a great service. These apprentices could bring a new kind of truth into the film industry by involving themselves in productions of merit. They would bring about new dimensions in the art of filmmaking for white people to see, to enjoy and to comprehend.

So the project involving those fifteen apprentices was practical from the standpoint that it encouraged blacks to get into fun, well-paying professions. The project was also social in that it encouraged the young apprentices to send their ideas out to the public. By forming their own production company they were in essence agreeing to project some of their own visions into the medium of film. This is essentially what Belafonte himself did when he formed his own production organization. Harry, beginning with *The World, The Flesh and The Devil,* was concentrating on producing films with ideas that were important to him and to blacks.

Harry, in discussing his apprentices, explained that the progress went beyond just finding jobs for a handful of blacks. The apprentices were not concerned just with finding employment in the movie industry. They were very much concerned with what they would be saying and doing as creative people. These apprentices concerned with "black reality" would not be interested in doing silly, meaningless movies.

This effect, the Ford Foundation grant, and working with the apprentices, represented in 1969 the new black thrust toward equality in the film industry. Perhaps the original dream of a black, based on ego, might be to achieve stardom. However, it is more realistic and more important to the black community that these people learn how to get behind the cameras, handle the scripts and budget the films. The action is behind the scene as well as in the spotlight. More important, there is money in all areas of filmmaking. These millions of dollars can go back into the black community. The thrust of Belafonte's program was to teach blacks all areas of filmmaking, encouraging them to form their own companies and do their own films.

The next film in which Belafonte became involved, both as an actor and producer, was *Buck and The Preacher,* released in 1972. The production cost $2.5 million. Columbia Pictures put up the money and got distribution rights for the film. Sidney Poitier played the role of Buck and also was co-producer (E&R). Poitier also directed the film. Belafonte played the role of the Preacher and was also co-producer.

Buck and The Preacher was shot in Durango, Mexico. The town, northwest of Mexico City, was once a mining village. Now Durango is a location for moviemakers who want to make westerns at low cost. Poitier and Belafonte made this film hoping to follow it with others. The story is taken from real life. There was a band of ex-slaves called the Exodusters who traveled across the West looking for a new start after the Civil War. Drake Walker was the name of the young black writer who found the story of the Exodusters. Poitier had the script reworked by Ernest Kinoy, who had written his last movie, *Brother John.*

The story is not only a western with black cowboys, but it has some unusual incidents, variations on the regular western. There is a black-white shoot-out in a whorehouse, where the black men win. There is also a Third World agreement between blacks and American Indians against the "yellow hairs." Sidney Poitier is Buck, a fictional U.S. Cavalry veteran who leads a group all the way from Louisiana to Colorado, where they hope to find a new beginning. Finally, he is stopped by white vigilantes. Julie Robinson Belafonte, Harry's wife, plays the part of an Indian interpreter who is able to help Buck barter with the chief.

Buck is a man of impeccable personal conduct. He doesn't smoke or drink and he remains faithful to his woman. Ruby Dee plays his woman in the film. However, *Look* magazine, in its article of August 24, 1971, seemed to feel that Poitier was almost too cool in the movie. *Look* wrote that Poitier, established as a superactor, was yearning to secure his credentials as a filmmaker. In this film, he made his debut as a director—his biggest conquest since he won the Oscar for his performance in *Lilies of the Field*.

The magazine article claimed that while Poitier was busy watching camera angles with eyes in back of his head, "Belafonte may be stealing a movie." The description of Belafonte, who got rid of his matinee-idol image for the film, learning how to chew and spit tobacco and blacking out his teeth, was that of a funky, unwashed man. "For the part," wrote *Look,* "Belafonte, Mr. Hot, scraps that burdensome facade that made him a clean-cut mulatto sex symbol a decade ago." He was funky and pragmatic in *Buck and The Preacher,* looking scruffy and hungry. The article went on to say that Belafonte as the Preacher artfully "toms" for white men and black. In the film, Belafonte drank, chewed tobacco and wanted to womanize. He carried a gun inside his black, hollowed-out Bible. *Look* made a comment that had been made before about Belafonte: "Harry wanted to be recognized as a serious actor more than anything else in life." This quote in the article, page 57, came from a statement said to have been made by Mike Merrick, a close friend of Belafonte's and a business associate for more than 17 years.

The agreement from reviewers was that Belafonte did an excellent acting job in this film. One reviewer stated that Belafonte overacted in the film, that he was outrageous and very amusing. Another critic wrote that Belafonte was superb. Another critic was happy to see that Harry, for the first time in his career, with his blacked-out teeth, could show his skill as an actor. He was, in *Buck and The Preacher,* a good black actor, not just a good-looking black man with a nice voice.

Another critic said Belafonte had stolen the show with a wild and entertaining comic characterization. This critic felt that the comic characterization had been done so well by Belafonte that it might even be of Academy Award caliber among acting performances for the year. Vincent Canby, writing for the *New York Times* on April 29, 1972, stated that the movie was stolen almost at the start by Belafonte as a bogus preacher. Mr. Canby felt that Harry had mellowed considerably since his days as a matinee idol in such movies as *Island In The Sun.* Canby felt Belafonte's performance in *Buck* was only limited by the fact that the material in the film was simple.

Belafonte was described as a high-spirited con artist with bad teeth, a gaping eye and some dark memories which gave the film a few moments of dramatic distinction. *Variety* wrote that Belafonte was extremely versatile in the role. When Harry entered the scene the mood of the story lightened and changed to adventure and comedy. Poitier and Belafonte were likened to Butch and Sundance. *Variety* stated that Julie Belafonte was impressive in her part as an Indian maiden. But, it was really Belafonte who dominated the film.

There was a lot of talk surrounding the filming of *Buck and The Preacher*. Part of the interest in the film came from the fact that Belafonte and Poitier were attempting to make a film together. Some said that the two men were more rivals than friends. Their stories go back to the days at the American Negro Theater workshop, where they both had their beginnings as actors. However, not only was there controversy as to whether the long-time friends were really friends, but there was also a controversy about the directorship of the film. This did not involve Belafonte, but it had to do with Poitier and the original director of the film, Joe Sargent.

One week after the crew arrived in Durango to film *Buck and The Preacher,* the director was fired. Supposedly he was let go because he was shooting as if the film were being made for TV. The story goes that after filming for a week, Poitier paid Joe Sargent, gave a party in his honor, and sent him back to Los Angeles. The producers had decided that they really needed a black man to direct the film. It was a sensitive job requiring a sensitivity toward blacks. Since Poitier understood what was needed and how to get what he wanted, he became director, as well as star and producer.

Poitier was accused of having planned the whole thing before arriving on location. He denied having done any such thing, saying that the director was a friend of his. Poitier contended that he didn't have to sacrifice other people to get where he wanted to go. Whatever the true story, the incident created talk, which along with the stories of rivalry between Belafonte and Poitier, made the filming of *Buck and The Preacher* of interest for more than just the film itself.

People are always interested in stories about show-business personalities. Just as the country read with interest the tales about Harry's divorce from his first wife and his marriage to Julie Robinson, they were interested in a story about rivalry between Academy Award-winning Sidney Poitier and handsome matinee idol and international singing star, Harry Belafonte. *Look* titled the article on the two: "Durango: Poitier meets Belafonte; Two wary rivals patch up a fight to make a movie together."

There were stories constantly going around in the show business world about Harry's rivalry with Belafonte. There was one tale about a disagreement they had when they were in Atlanta just after the funeral of Dr. Martin Luther King. Sidney accused Harry of trying to run the show. Someone described them as exhibiting something close to sibling rivalry.

It was pointed out how unusual their lives have been, how out of the ordinary. It was suggested that, in 1964 when Poitier received the Academy Award for best actor in the film *Lilies of The Field,* there were indeed few blacks who could stand beside him. Belafonte was one of the few. There just weren't that many blacks who had risen to the heights that Belafonte and Poitier had. The night Poitier received the Oscar, he talked of having made a long journey. When Poitier arrived at the top, there were few blacks to greet him. Also, it just happens that money changes people, separates them from one another. Men who don't have money and men who have lots of money tend to separate for various reasons. Thus, having someone like Belafonte around, rich also, was necessary to Poitier so that he would not stand alone. It is not just the money; it is the power and influence that go along with it. Life changes when there is so much power and money. If Belafonte and Poitier sometimes looked like cautious jungle animals stalking around each other, it is because they had reached such heights, where there was money and power, along with a lot of envy and competition.

When Poitier and Belafonte both started in the Forties neither of them had anything but ambition. Poitier's West Indian accent was so strong that he was asked not to stay around the American Negro Theater workshop. While Belafonte continued to show up at the workshop and move scenery, taking small acting jobs, earning a living as a maintenance worker in Harlem, Sidney bought a cheap radio. He listened to his radio and practiced his accent. Also, being a young man with burning ambition, he continued to show up at the ANT workshop and eventually was accepted.

They both went to the drama school, which Marlon Brando attended. Then, through hard work and a blinding, driving ambition, the two men rose to stardom. The climb up the ladder, the rejections and the strength it must have taken, are only things Belafonte and Poitier

Ten Powerful Years

would understand. Poitier had worked in the garment center while trying to find acting work. Harry, on the verge of doing the same thing, had been launched into a singing career.

Stories about their rivalry are common. But, stories about their friendship are common too. If their relationship does sometimes resemble that of brothers, then the love-hate quality would make sense. When Harry did a TV show, a spectacular called "The Strollin' '20s," he asked Sidney to join him, and Poitier did. People who saw them together and knew them said they acted as usual, like sibling rivals.

The story goes that when the two were in Atlanta, after the funeral of Martin Luther King, their rivalry burst open. They were both close to the dead civil rights leader and both of them were asked to help the Southern Christian Leadership Conference raise funds. It is said that the two began to bicker. It is reported that Sidney accused Harry of trying to run things, telling him to shut up. Then Harry was offended and the two stopped speaking.

Of course, Sidney was the first person Harry turned to when he found a movie script he liked, just as when Belafonte was hosting the "Tonight Show" he asked Poitier to make an appearance. The "fight" after King's death had to be tabled so that the movie script could be discussed. They made up because Harry wanted Sidney to see the script. Harry could trust Sidney to give his opinion honestly about the film script. Of course, the script was for *Buck and The Preacher*.

Sidney and Ernest Kinoy revised and polished the script while Harry worked at shaping his character.

Then Harry tried getting money for the film, but Sidney finally was able to get the financing. Although Sidney is said to have offered Harry co-star billing, Harry refused because he felt that Sidney was the film star with the track record. In spite of the egos they are said to both have, they got through the planning without any major problems.

There were, however, rumors that the feuding started again while filming in Durango. One story goes that Poitier called Belafonte "boy." There was a rumor that Sidney left Harry's birthday party early, not staying to hear Harry finish singing with the mariachis. Someone noted that this must have hurt Harry's feelings. Then there was the thing about Harry, who thought it was fashionable to be late. There was a rumor of a hassle between the two about Harry showing up late to see the rushes of the film. Perhaps, someone suggested, Harry figured a star had the right to be late. The story goes that he came in late every night during the filming of *Buck*. After everyone had seen the rushes, the projectionist had to start all over for Belafonte. One night it is told that Belafonte asked Poitier to wait until he got there to show the rushes. Poitier said "sure," but the next night started the rushes just before Belafonte walked in late. Poitier was letting Belafonte know that he was second in *Buck and The Preacher*.

Stories about the two of them go on and on. They say that they're too close for rivalry. On *Buck*, if Harry got any credit, Poitier would share in it and vice versa.

What it comes down to, perhaps, is that they had their petty grievances. Both Belafonte and Poitier were known to have big egos. Yet, when Belafonte needed someone good to do a film with him or appear on a TV show, he called Poitier. Poitier seemed to do the same with Belafonte. They are both superstars. They are also both obsessive, hard working men. During the filming of *Buck and The Preacher,* conditions were not the best. In Durango the nights were freezing and the days scorching. The food in Mexico made everyone sick and there was the daily grueling schedule.

However, Poitier was up before dawn with energy and enthusiasm. He liked his work. For nine weeks Poitier and Belafonte worked six days a week and a half day on Sunday. Poitier was known for taking his vitamins and lack of interest in alcohol or pills. Belafonte has always been known as a light drinker. They are too concerned with getting the work down right to indulge in counter-productive behavior. The cast of *Buck* was mostly black. The conditions, no heat in the rooms and vegetables which might make you sick, were certainly not the best.

Poitier worked like a madman through the unpleasant conditions. Neither Belafonte nor Poitier are known to let much of themselves out to people. They are private men. Perhaps they did have petty differences, but they could not have been too bad. After the completion of the filming of *Buck and The Preacher,* Poitier and Belafonte teamed up again for the filming *Uptown Saturday Night.*

The Sixties and beginning of the Seventies showed Belafonte as active as ever. If he indicated a concern about the longevity of his career in 1959, his concern seems to have been for naught. In August of 1971, when the *Look* magazine article on *Buck and The Preacher,* was published, Belafonte was shown to be going strong as ever. He was in his forties at that time. Appearing on TV shows, maintaining an active concert schedule and producing and starring in films with Poitier was as good an indication as any that his career indeed would have longevity. There is very definitely a "Poitier power" and a "Belafonte power."

Chapter Thirteen
Lord Harry, the Actor

Belafonte, now well into the third decade of his fabulous career, made the film *Uptown Saturday Night,* released in 1974. The reviews on this film, again directed by Poitier, were not so good. The movie contained top stars—Bill Cosby, Belafonte, Flip Wilson, Richard Pryor and Roscoe Lee Brown.

Billed as a black comedy by Warner Brothers and a release of First Artists Productions, the film was described by *Variety* as a "disappointingly uneven comedy." The criticism was of a bad screenplay, bad performances and bad direction.

The story dealt with a high-spirited taxi driver, Wardell Franklin (Bill Cosby), who persuaded his shy friend Steve Jackson (Sidney Poitier), a factory worker, to spend a Saturday night at an exclusive gambling club called Madame Zenobia's. While they were having fun the club was raided by some masked men who stole everyone's valuables including Steve's winning lottery ticket. Not trusting the police, Steve and Wardell decided to find the crooks themselves. After a phony private detective, Sharp Eye Washington (Richard Pryor), made off with the fee Steve paid him, the two asked Congressman Lincoln (Roscoe Lee Brown) for help and found out that the Congressman's wife, Leggy Peggy (Paula Kelly), was an habitue of Madame Zenobia's.

Leggy Peggy put them in touch with hood Little Seymour (Harold Nicholas), who then led them to Greechie Dan Beauford (Belafonte), a big-time gangster at the time involved in organizing a gang war against his rival, Silky Slim (Calvin Lockhart). Steve and Wardell recognized by something he said that Slim was the leader of the raid on Zenobia's. They concocted an elaborate plan to get back the ticket and have all the gangsters arrested at the same time.

Both gangs assembled at a charity picnic. The police swooped in and got them all except Slim, who tried to escape with the ticket in his suitcase. Steve went after him and they struggled. The suitcase got tossed off a high bridge. Both Steve and Wardell dove into the river to retrieve the ticket.

There was varied criticism about the film, mostly not so good. One critic said this movie was an attempt to feature black people as characters other than supercool assassins. Unfortunately, this writer felt, had the movie been filmed with white actors and actresses, the old, dead comedy routines would resemble a farce of the Forties. The critic felt that the actors tried to affect a happy-go-lucky tone, but the material was so bad and Poitier's direction so uninspired that the performances looked depressingly mediocre. The critic saw *Uptown Saturday Night* as a big waste of talent.

Another critic felt that the assets of the film were the ragamuffin charm and few amusing bits by Cosby, Belafonte and some of the others. However, most reviews felt that there was not enough inventive comedy. A zippier pace was needed. Belafonte's campy imitation of Brando's "Godfather" was considered good.

To date, this was the last film in which Belafonte acted. However, there were almost ten years between *Odds Against Tomorrow* and *The Angel Levine,* so it is hard to tell what Belafonte's plans are as far as films are concerned. He is only in his early fifties, and there are people like Bob Hope and George Burns acting up a storm in their seventies and eighties, so Belafonte's film career could go in many directions.

Belafonte remained in the Seventies and still is today, at the onset of the Eighties, very interested in civil rights for blacks and all people. *Jet* ran an article on April 29, 1979, about Harry's participation in a campaign to re-elect the black reform mayor, Richard G. Hatcher, of Gary, Indiana. Harry, along with Sammy Davis Jr., Bill Cosby and Dick Gregory, went to the aid of their man, feeling that he stood for the things for which Martin Luther King had struggled.

Speaking to the audience at a benefit rally for Mayor Hatcher, Belafonte revealed his deep commitment to helping blacks. *Jet* quoted him as saying:

"I am often told that as an artist, I should concern myself with only the field of art, and not involve myself with politics. . . . But since I am a man, since I am black, since I am a father having children and a wife, I've found that there is nothing that happens politically that does not affect me and my family; does not affect me and my blackness."

Belafonte and the other black entertainers were attempting to gain support for Mayor Hatcher, who was seeking re-election in May of that year against Democratic organization-backed Dr. Alexander Williams, also black. Harry and the others were in Indiana to raise money and drum up support for Mayor Hatcher.

Harry had donated his talent in the previous campaign to help get Hatcher elected. However, as the opposition had become more cunning, it was necessary for Belafonte and the others to again lend a hand. *Jet* quoted Harry further: "In this instance the opposition has become much more panicky. Before, they gave us just the machine, and Richard (Hatcher) knew how to deal with that. Now they have cloaked the decay and the corruption of that machine with a cloak of color in the name of a black candidate who now runs on the opposition."

Belafonte felt very strongly about the worth of Mayor Hatcher. He also felt that Williams, who he didn't know, was in essence betraying a cause. Said Harry, according to *Jet,* "I did not know Hitler, I did not know Judas. I have known none of the great betrayers of history, but I know who they are and I know what they were. I know they must have been men of low substance."

Harry told the gathering that if any more campaign money for Hatcher were needed, he and the others would raise it. He added that if they couldn't raise the money then he would give it to them personally. Belafonte told the audience that he would do this, "Because I loved and trusted and worked with Martin Luther King Jr. during the years he gave the best of his manhood so that there would be a Richard G. Hatcher."

At a rally for Hatcher, Belafonte sang, Davis also sang, Cosby emceed and Gregory gave humor and political satire. *Jet* wrote that support was building for Hatcher across the nation. Many blacks wanted to see this reform mayor re-elected.

Thus Belafonte in the Seventies was not only involved in films and concerts, but was also giving his time and talent to help black causes. In an article entitled "Belafonte Bounces Back Big and Black," dated July, 1972, *Jet* described Belafonte as he was in the Seventies. The article not only wrote about the film, *Buck and The Preacher,* which had just been done by Harry and Sidney Poitier, but it also gave insight and depth to Belafonte's commitment to black causes.

The article, written by M. Cordell Thompson, stated that Belafonte was an indefatigable person. He was in his middle years, but he stood on the threshold of a new career as movie idol and preacher. *Jet* explained that Harry was still very successful as a singer, and that he had already done well as an actor, on both stage and screen. Mentioned as successes were *Carmen Jones,* which made lots of money, and *The Angel Levine,* in which Harry did a fine acting job. *Jet* brought up the fact that Harry, "a balladeer's balladeer," had the ability to move around on stage in an open-necked shirt and drive women crazy.

Jet then devoted several pages to a discussion of Belafonte's role in *Buck and The Preacher* and what the black western was going to be able to do for Belafonte and other blacks. However, the main thrust of the *Jet* article was on Belafonte's interests, insofar as they concerned black subjects. Harry said he and Sidney were doing their homework, so that they as producers and moviemakers could present black history in a way never dreamed of before.

Both Poitier and Belafonte were extremely interested in the blacks of Africa in 1972. On a trip which they took to the African continent, they met with the president of Tanzania and the president of Zambia to make plans about the making of films in Africa which would be about Africans and Afro-Americans.

They felt that if their efforts worked out they would not only be helping unfold black history, but they would be bringing money into Africa. They could use Africa's resources to unfold the interpretations of the African theme. Harry and Sidney as individuals represented to the Africans some of the skills that blacks had to offer. If Belafonte and Poitier were able to work out the business details, they would be able to shoot black reality and history much more cheaply in Africa than they could in the States. In turn, using African industries would put money into Africa. Also, using their people would develop their industries, institutions and craftsmen. The world would be able to see an image of Africa and its history.

Belafonte claims to have received much help both as a man and as an artist from blacks, whether through knowing them personally or following their examples.

Lord Harry, the Actor

The giants in black history were of help to him during the long, difficult road he had to climb in order to succeed. Harry said that the first two most powerful influences in his life were Dr. Du Bois and Paul Robeson.

However, Belafonte felt it was Dr. King who had been the real positive black influence in his life. King had helped Harry and other blacks learn to channel their anger and violence. *Jet* quoted Belafonte as saying: "And when it came to the time of Dr. King, I was terribly angry and wounded. I was a wounded beast like so many others looking for vengeance." But King had a sense of history and a commitment to the black condition. He was able to show Harry, "that there was a larger humanity than anything my anger could imagine." This is how Belafonte learned to redirect hostility into a positive thrust—working for black destiny. Belafonte felt that still, even after the death of King, non-violence was worthwhile.

Belafonte pointed out that also because of King, there were, in 1972, over 2,400 elected black officials in the country, whereas before King, there were only 300. The move toward electoral politics came out of the King era, he feels. As Harry said in the previous *Jet* article dealing with his need for involvement in politics because as a black man he wanted to be involved, in this article Belafonte spoke out for black conventions, black political platforms. He felt that with black conventions, platforms would be gotten together which would be of help to black causes and would cross political lines.

Harry felt, since they were a minority vote in the Democratic Party, that blacks should be independent enough of the Democratic Party to be the minority vote for anything. He felt they should know how to use their minority power shrewdly, with both Democrats and Republicans.

Jet also reported in this article how Belafonte took time out from his busy concert schedule to help in prisons. He does concerts in prisons because he is interested in the Martin Luther King, Jr. Center for Social Change. Also, Belafonte believes in using his popularity toward what he feels strongly committed to, what he feels are the main needs of the black community.

Jet quoted Belafonte as saying: "Most of the individuals who are in prison are there as a result of the consciousness that flowed out of civil rights. The revolutionary is behind bars because he has revolutionary ideas and has been at odds with the old thrust liberationist who started with SNCC, SCLC, CORE, NAACP and the Urban League. There are other blacks behind bars because they wanted to be involved with finer things."

Belafonte was quoted by *Jet* as saying that prison revolts are a new level of consciousness, an assertiveness. Belafonte also became involved with a group in Los Angeles, California, called the Harriet Tubman Bookshelf. This organization was a social and political study center for the families of prisoners. The point was to encourage families to send prisoners things to help them redirect and refine their energies, so that when the prisoners were released, instead of returning to crime they would be able to turn toward a better destiny.

Belafonte was also quoted as being happy that black legislators were helping to change and better prison conditions.

Lord Harry, the Actor

Harry Belafonte in 1972 was known to be a very wealthy man. He said in the *Jet* article that he planned to leave a decent amount of his wealth to his wife and children but, "the rest goes into institutions, because I believe that we have to close the gap between us and the white man."

The article closed with a strong statement of commitment from Belafonte. It is hard to reconcile the following quote with the statement made in 1959 by a critic that Belafonte wished he were white. In the *Jet* article, Harry is quoted as saying: "Every black artist, every black for that matter, should ask themselves what is their commitment. Get into that. Use whatever platform you have to interpret the West Indies, to interpret the ghettos. If you're a big powerful black cat, go find a Miriam Makeba, or a Letta Mbulu and let them stand up on the stage with you and sing of their Africaness. If you're a writer, dig into the heart of Africa and find out where the drama is and unfold it on the stage and in our churches. And if you feel you've got something to say, then rap."

The magnificent thing about the talent and energy of Belafonte is that he feels strongly about his race, volunteers to do concerts in prisons, protests for civil rights, supports black candidates such as Hatcher, and still has the energy to do concerts in the States and in Europe, breaking box-office records and raking in astronomical amounts of money. If he was making lots of money on concert tours in the 1950s, he still pulled it in in the '60s and '70s. *Variety* reported on Wednesday, December 1, 1976, "Belafonte Wraps Europe With a $1-mil Take."

In 1976, Belafonte toured Europe from October 19 to

November 14, giving 27 concerts. In all, he played to 39,000 people and took in a gross of $1,000,000. Singing in Scandanavia, West Germany, Switzerland, Austria, The Netherlands, Belgium and France, he packed the concert houses. All houses, most of which seated 2000, were sold out a week before showtime. *Variety* quoted the average ticket price as being $25.00.

The interesting fact is that according to *Variety*, Harry had not toured Europe in over fifteen years. He was also scheduled to again tour Europe in 1977.

In the United States, in February, 1977, Belafonte was given excellent reviews at Caesar's Palace in Las Vegas. Perhaps what *Jet* said about Belafonte in 1972, the fact that he was in his "middle years," had nothing to do with his showbusiness ability. That he was indefatigable was proving true. Harry had been a hit in Vegas in the mid-Fifties. This was already the late Seventies, over twenty years later.

Variety noted that Harry had not played Vegas since the summer of '74. He was back in January 1977 with "another of his top drawer presentations." *Variety* wrote that Harry's distinctive tones were again used to interpret Belafonte-type tunes.

In the Fall of 1977, Belafonte was again touring Europe. It was reported that, in spite of the price of the tickets, which were as high as $42.00, the show in Zurich was a sellout. This made it evident that the Swiss public was willing to shell out big prices if the show or the personality warranted the expense.

Not only was the show a sellout, but at the end of his performance, which lasted nearly three hours, the audience shouted for more. The reactions to the performer were strong all through the show. *Variety* reported that

Lord Harry, the Actor

this 1977 tour was from September 23 to November 12, and included twenty-six cities in Germany, Switzerland, France, Holland, Sweden, Norway and Denmark, finishing with England.

The story of Belafonte is an ongoing tale. When he played the Greek Theater in Los Angeles in the summer of 1979, he was well received, as always.

Harry Belafonte's checkerboard career has brilliantly spanned several decades. He has proved to be a survivor in an industry—show business—where fame is as difficult to achieve as it is usually short-lived. What's more, Belafonte is no less controversial today than he was when he first burst upon the entertainment scene some thirty-odd years ago. Moreover, he is still pretty much the man of mystery that he always has been, as the following pages will show.

Which leads this particular biographer to point out that if there are several familiar features that keep surfacing throughout Belafonte's many-faceted career, they would have to be controversy, pioneering and mystery. Some random examples are in order:

In the 1940s Belafonte was an unglamorous maintenance man in Harlem, yet only ten years later he became "the World's First Black Matinee Idol," as sought after by white women as he was by black women. The circumstances that brought him to such unique prominence are bizarre and without precedent. There are some people in the business who feel he may have pushed a little too hard to become a star, allegedly hurting many friends and associates in the process. You will be able to judge for yourself what is true and false about these accusations.

Paradoxically, Belafonte labored hard and relentlessly to become the leading calypso singer of his time. But when the media continually referred to him as "the King of Calypso," he grew incensed and strove not to be identified with that title. Why?

Then there's the sensitive business surrounding his two marriages. Belafonte divorced his first wife of many years to marry a beautiful white dancer. A large contingent of his peers and the press vilified him for leaving his first wife for a white woman. On the other hand, others praised him for his courage to defy convention and listen to his heart. What are the true circumstances attached to this agonizing period in Belafonte's life? For the first time *all* the facts about both marriages are brought to light in these pages.

Controversy stormed through his life again when he became the first black star to play the romantic lead opposite a white actress in a major motion picture, *Island In The Sun*—a film that caused rioting and picketing throughout the South. He was simultaneously hailed as a "black Valentino" and damned as an "uppity nigger" for daring to appear as the lover of a white woman in a movie. What did such contradictory commentary do to Belafonte's self-image at that juncture in his life? The answers are as insightful as they are disturbing.

Belafonte was a close personal friend of Martin Luther King and one of the early Peace Marchers and champions of the whole Civil Rights Movement back in the Fifties. Yet some critics accused Belafonte of being an Uncle Tom and hostile to the NAACP. One newspaper went so far as to accuse him of wanting to be

Lord Harry, the Actor

white. On the other hand there were white and black observers of the political and entertainment scene who said Belafonte capitalized on his blackness to get ahead, that he was too militantly pro-black. What is the truth behind these contradictions?

Then there's the cloud of rumors, innuendos and outright criticisms hanging over his relationships with friends and business associates. As just one example from many, Belafonte's ongoing feud with the equally famous actor Sidney Poitier has become common knowledge. It's strange, too, because their lives have overlapped many times. They co-produced and starred together in *Buck and The Preacher*. These two black giants of the entertainment industry first met as paupers in their youth and hit stardom about the same time. They were also dedicated activists during the Civil Rights Movement of the Fifties and they worked together in many capacities. With so many similarities in background and aspirations, logic dictates that they should always have been close friends. Nothing, however, could be farther from the truth. What is the underlying cause of their longstanding rivalry? By the time you finish reading this book you should have a deeper understanding of the Belafonte-Poitier feud.

Still another mystery about Belafonte confronts us, and it relates to him as a world-famous singer. Belafonte was the first artist to record an LP album for RCA Victor to sell over a million copies. Over the years, literally millions of his fans in America and Europe have crowded concerts, stadium halls and the most prestigious nightclubs and theaters in the world to see and hear him sing. Yet he has never been entirely comfortable with his singer's persona, fancying himself more of an actor and intellectual than a singer—even though his credits as an actor or intellectual force pale beside his smashing successes and permanently entrenched position as a singer. Why does Belafonte resist accepting his universally acknowledged role as a singer par excellence?

Perhaps by now you have some glimmer of how difficult it is to explain the richness of Harry Belafonte. Singer, actor, linguist, political force. Father. A sex-object whose sex appeal transcends the color line. Business entrepreneur. Egotist. Humanitarian. These are only a handful of the many facets of Belafonte's complex personality. And even more examples of his many-sidedness will not only be revealed in the ensuing pages, they will be more clearly defined than ever before.

By the time you finish reading this Harry Belafonte biography, you will have had all the aforementioned questions answered, along with whatever else you wish to know about this truly fascinating man and great artist—a man whose creative presence is still very much felt in many vital areas of our society.

This book attempts to graphically illustrate how one talented and determined black youth overcame crippling social, economic, racial and professional obstacles to become one of the all-time show business greats. And in demonstrating how Belafonte became the star he still is today, his life becomes a blueprint of escape for other minority members who long to rise above the shabby circumstances into which they were born.

From unpaid stagehand to calypso singer to screen star par excellence, the inspirational career of Harry

Lord Harry, the Actor

Belafonte shines forth as *the* modern edifice to the black man's will to create and succeed in the crucible of racial discrimination and professional antagonism. During his dynamic career Belafonte has been called King of Calypso, balladeer, blues singer, matinee idol, dramatic actor of stage and screen and movie mogul. But the goal of the real Belafonte has always been to avoid being pinned down and stereotyped. His life force continues to drive him from one creative project to another, leaving in his wake a world changed for the better by the magic Belafonte touch. He may deny being the King of Calypso, but he'll understand when we call him Lord Harry, The Actor.

DISCOGRAPHY

Unless otherwise noted, all of the albums listed below were on the RCA Victor label.

MARK TWAIN and other folk favorites (1954)

BELAFONTE (1956)

CALYPSO (1956)

AN EVENING WITH BELAFONTE (1957)

BELAFONTE SINGS OF THE CARIBBEAN (1957)

TO WISH YOU A MERRY CHRISTMAS (1958)

BELAFONTE SINGS THE BLUES (1958)

LOVE IS A GENTLE THING (1959)

PORGY AND BESS Harry Belafonte and Lena Horne (1959)

BELAFONTE AT CARNEGIE HALL (1959)

MY LORD WHAT A MORNIN' (1960)

BELAFONTE SINGS BLUES (1960)

SWING DAT HAMMER (1960)

BELAFONTE RETURNS TO CARNEGIE HALL (1960)

JUMP UP CALYPSO (1961)

MANY MOODS (1962)

BALLADS, BLUES (1964)

BELAFONTE AT THE GREEK THEATER (1964)

AN EVENING WITH MAKEBA (1965)

EVENING WITH MOUSKOURI (1966)

IN MY QUIET ROOM (1966)

CALYPSO IN BRASS (1966)

THIS IS HARRY BELAFONTE (1970)

BY REQUEST (1970)

HOMEWARD BOUND (1970)

WARM TOUCH (1971)

CALYPSO CARNIVAL (1971)

BELAFONTE LIVE (1972)

PLAY ME (1974)

HARRY (1974, Camden)

PURE GOLD (1975)

ABRAHAM, MARTIN AND JOHN (1975, Camden)

MIDNIGHT (1978)

BELAFONTE LEGENDARY (1978)

FILMS

THE BRIGHT ROAD MGM 1953
with: Harry Belafonte, Dorothy Dandridge, Philip Hepburn

CARMEN JONES FOX 1954
with: Dorothy Dandridge, Harry Belafonte, Pearl Bailey, Olga James

ISLAND IN THE SUN FOX 1957
with: Harry Belafonte, James Mason, Joan Fontaine, Dorothy Dandridge, Joan Collins, Michael Rennie, Stephen Boyd

THE WORLD, THE FLESH AND THE DEVIL MGM 1959
with: Harry Belafonte, Inger Stevens, Mel Ferrer

ODDS AGAINST TOMORROW UA 1959
with: Harry Belafonte, Robert Ryan, Shelly Winters

THE ANGEL LEVINE UA 1970
with: Harry Belafonte, Zero Mostel, Ida Kaminski, Gloria Foster

BUCK AND THE PREACHER Columbia 1972
with: Harry Belafonte, Sidney Poitier, Cameron Mitchell, Ruby Dee, Julie Belafonte

UPTOWN SATURDAY NIGHT Warner 1974
with: Harry Belafonte, Sidney Poitier, Bill Cosby, Flip Wilson, Richard Pryor, Rosalind Cash, Roscoe Lee Browne, Paula Kelly, Lee Chamberlin

ABOUT THE AUTHOR

Genia Fogelson took her masters degree in French literature at New York University in 1967, then went to Jackson, Mississippi, where she taught comparative literature at Tougaloo College and other institutions for four years during that period of racial crisis.

Ms. Fogelson began freelance writing in 1977 and has published her novel, *Jewel: Undercover Cop* (Holloway House, 1979), as well as several articles in *Players* and other popular magazines.

Genia currently resides in an apartment overlooking the yacht basin in Marina del Rey, California, where she is at work on her doctoral dissertation on French filmwriter and novelist Marguerite Duras and various freelance projects. Her hobbies are tennis and travel.

BEHIND THE HOLLYWOOD GLITTER
SEX—DRUGS—VIOLENCE

FICTION / In this, her first novel, actress Carol Speed has drawn upon her own filmmaking experience to open the curtains on the inner workings of Black Hollywood. ■ For Dorothy Dickerson, rising young black film actress, stardom was her only goal and she was prepared to do anything to achieve success. *The Chance,* her new film, provided the opportunity she had been waiting for. And Dorothy had an extra advantage—Fred Sullivan, underworld figure, player supreme and the money behind *The Chance.* Dorothy tied her star to Fred's, with tragic results.

BH006 - $2.25

HOLLOWAY HOUSE PUBLISHING CO.
8060 MELROSE AVE., LOS ANGELES, CALIF. 90046

Gentlemen: I enclose $_____ ____ ☐ cash, ☐ check, ☐ money order, payment in full for books ordered. I understand that if I am not completely satisfied, I may return my order within 10 days for a complete refund. (Add 50¢ per order to cover postage and handling. California residents add 6% tax. Please allow three weeks for delivery.)

☐ **BH006 INSIDE BLACK HOLLYWOOD $2.25**

Name_____

Address_____

City_____ State_____ Zip_____

HE FOUGHT MANY BATTLES BUT HIS BIGGEST WERE OUTSIDE THE RING

JOE LOUIS
BIOGRAPHY OF A CHAMPION
BY RUGIO VITALE

BIOGRAPHY / He was the most loved heavyweight boxing champion of all times and the greatest. Millions of words have been written about him but none, until now, have been able to capture his warmth as a human being and the stress in the world in which he lived. This is the story of Joe Louis, a simple boy from the red clay hills of Alabama who rose from poverty to gain immortality none before him had ever achieved. With his fame came personal and political monsters that would never leave him until he was completely broken. But he would not break. The millions who loved him rallied to his side. There is history in this book but, above all, there is a man.

HOLLOWAY HOUSE PUBLISHING CO.
8060 MELROSE AVE., LOS ANGELES, CALIF. 90046

Gentlemen: I enclose $_____ ☐ cash, ☐ check, ☐ money order, payment in full for books ordered. I understand that if I am not completely satisfied, I may return my order within 10 days for a complete refund. (Add 50¢ per order to cover postage and handling. California residents add 6% tax. Please allow three weeks for delivery.)

☐ BH655, JOE LOUIS, BIOGRAPHY OF A CHAMPION, $1.95

Name_____

Address_____

City_____ State_____ Zip_____

HIS MUSIC MADE HIM AN IMMORTAL WHO LIVES ON IN THE HEART OF MANKIND

LOUIS ARMSTRONG
BIOGRAPHY OF A MUSICIAN
by ROBERT HOSKINS

He found his life's passion when he was living in the Home for Colored Waifs in his hometown of New Orleans and began playing a battered old trumpet. Soon he was playing those sweet, often salty, notes in every funeral parade, every honky-tonk and "parlor" in New Orleans' famed Storyville. ■ But New Orleans soon proved to be too small a pond for this king of jazz. Satchmo headed north, first to Chicago, where the legend began to grow, then on to Harlem where his fame mushroomed. From there he conquered the world with his music. ■ Women problems, bad management, traditional prejudice and criticism from his own people plagued the father of jazz for many years. But he survived, met his challenges with characteristic forthrightness, and always came out on top. ■ Brilliant writing by author Robert Hoskins makes this must-read book a delightful entertainment. His word pictures of Satchmo, the man, of New Orleans and Harlem are fascinating, priceless. This is a big book. You'll enjoy the experience.

HOLLOWAY HOUSE PUBLISHING CO.
8060 MELROSE AVE., LOS ANGELES, CALIF. 90046

Gentlemen: I enclose $_____ ☐ cash, ☐ check, ☐ money order, payment in full for books ordered. I understand that if I am not completely satisfied, I may return my order within 10 days for a complete refund. (Add 50¢ per order to cover postage and handling. California residents add 6% tax. Please allow three weeks for delivery.)

BH668, LOUIS ARMSTRONG, $1.95

Name_____

Address_____

City_____ State_____ Zip_____

ANDREW YOUNG
BIOGRAPHY OF A REALIST

BY EDDIE STONE

BIOGRAPHY / Impatient and frustrated in his efforts to secure world peace and justice, Andrew Young resigned his post as U.S. ambassador to the United Nations after a breach of protocol embarrassed Israeli-American policy over the Palestine Liberation Organization. But that step in his career should prove to be only a pause in his meteoric rise to world prominence. Young's life has been characterized by his work for the good of all men, although his beginnings would not have presaged his life to come. After giving up an uninvolved middle class existence to become a minister, Andrew Young joined forces with Martin Luther King to fight on the front lines of the civil rights movement, quickly becoming a respected black leader in is own right. Credited with delivering the black vote for President Carter in 1976, Young will undoubtedly continue to have a powerful influence in the world political arena for many years to come. Andrew Young—realist, mediator, and spokesman for his people—is above all a fascinating character brought into sharp focus by author Eddie Stone.

HOLLOWAY HOUSE PUBLISHING CO.
8060 MELROSE AVE., LOS ANGELES, CALIF. 90046

Gentlemen: I enclose $_____ ☐ cash, ☐ check, ☐ money order, payment in full for books ordered. I understand that if I am not completely satisfied, I may return my order within 10 days for a complete refund. (Add 50¢ per order to cover postage and handling. California residents add 6% tax. Please allow three weeks for delivery.)

☐ BH673, ANDREW YOUNG, BIOGRAPHY OF A REALIST, $1.95

Name_____

Address_____

City_____ State_____ Zip_____

PAUL ROBESON
BIOGRAPHY OF A PROUD MAN
BY JOSEPH NAZEL

BIOGRAPHY / Paul Robeson—proud, defiant, beloved, reviled, misunderstood, idolized—was above all a man of principle, whose deep and abiding love for his people was the driving force in his life. ■ By refusing to play the stereotypical roles offered him by Hollywood, he spurned fabulous riches available to very few of his race. By championing the rights of black people the world over and recognizing their roots in Africa years before the word Afro-American was coined, he created controversy that swirled around his head for decades. By defying the infamous House on Un-American Activities Committee, he proved the power of his principles while dooming himself to an ever-diminishing income. Even after death, controversy continued over his star in Hollywood's Walk of Fame. ■ Overcoming racial prejudice was more important to him than material considerations, even though his lifelong crusade to stamp out racism ultimately cost him his career and his health. But his pride remained intact until the very end. He became a legend in his own time and remains today a hero to black people the world over.

HOLLOWAY HOUSE PUBLISHING CO.
8060 MELROSE AVE., LOS ANGELES, CALIF. 90046

Gentlemen: I enclose $_____ ☐ cash, ☐ check, ☐ money order, payment in full for books ordered. I understand that if I am not completely satisfied, I may return my order within 10 days for a complete refund. (Add 50¢ per order to cover postage and handling. California residents add 6% tax. Please allow three weeks for delivery.)

☐ BH652, PAUL ROBESON, BIOGRAPHY OF A PROUD MAN, $1.95

Name_____
Address_____
City_____ State_____ Zip_____

Knocks the lid off the lone assassin theory!

A Case of Conspiracy
by Michael Newton

JAMES EARL RAY AND THE ASSASSINATION OF MARTIN LUTHER KING, JR.

NONFICTION / On April 4, 1968, at 6:01 p.m., a shot rang out. The great civil rights leader, Rev. Martin Luther King Jr., fell to the floor with massive head and throat wounds. Death was almost instantaneous. After a manhunt that spanned the United States, Canada and Mexico, James Earl Ray was arrested sixty-five days later at London's Heathrow Airport and accused of being King's assassin. But was he? Only Ray's surprise guilty plea, which he later recanted, saved the prosecution from having to prove their case ■ ■ ■ In a carefully researched and gripping step-by-step reconstruction of the assassination and its aftermath, author Michael Newton raises new and troubling questions about the investigation, arrest and trial of James Earl Ray which suggest that a conspiracy did indeed exist and that Ray may not have been the assassin after all. In the process, the author exposes faulty investigative techniques, self-serving attorneys and most important, reveals James Earl Ray's character as never before. It's as exciting and puzzling as any mystery novel published in recent years.

HOLLOWAY HOUSE PUBLISHING CO.
8060 MELROSE AVE., LOS ANGELES, CALIF. 90046

Gentlemen: I enclose $_____ ☐ cash, ☐ check, ☐ money order, payment in full for books ordered. I understand that if I am not completely satisfied, I may return my order within 10 days for a complete refund. (Add 50¢ per order to cover postage and handling. California residents add 6% tax. Please allow three weeks for delivery.)

☐ BH003, A CASE OF CONSPIRACY, $1.95

Name _____

Address _____

City _____ State _____ Zip _____

She's beautiful, black, dangerous, and she's unforgettable! She's...

JEWEL
UNDERCOVER COP
by Genia Fogelson

FICTION / You may want to play games with Jewel Smith. She's young, black, beautiful and sensuous. But beware, she's an undercover cop with a taste for danger and the sting of a scorpion. Her assignment, the most dangerous of her career, is to pose as a high school biology teacher and apprehend a gang of youthful burglars and murderers who have been terrorizing the wealthy community of Marina del Rey. Her masquerade puts her in league with strange bedfellows, some deadly, all interesting, in a twisting, exotic plot full of surprises. She loses her partner, her informant, and comes very close to losing her own life several times. Then slowly she unravels the mystery surrounding Duke, Cobra, Goat and the rest of a gang called the *Hawks*, and of Big Earl and his man-eating panther, Satan. ■ This book is a shocker with gripping realism and surprise twists keeping you glued to your chair until the last page is turned. And long after the book is a distant memory, you'll remember Jewel Smith, the most exciting heroine ever ...

HOLLOWAY HOUSE PUBLISHING CO.
8060 MELROSE AVE., LOS ANGELES, CALIF. 90046

Gentlemen: I enclose $_____ ☐ cash, ☐ check, ☐ money order, payment in full for books ordered. I understand that if I am not completely satisfied, I may return my order within 10 days for a complete refund. (Add 50¢ per order to cover postage and handling. California residents add 6% tax. Please allow three weeks for delivery.)

☐ **BH665—JEWEL, UNDERCOVER COP, $1.95**

Name_____

Address_____

City_____ State_____ Zip_____

BOOK ORDER FORM

Dear Reader:

You'll find many other books of interest listed on previous pages. If they are not now available at your book dealer, we will be delighted to rush your order by direct mail. Fill in form below and mail with your remittance.

SPECIAL ORDER BOOK DEPT.
8060 MELROSE AVE. • LOS ANGELES, CALIF. 90046

Please send me the following books I have listed by Number. ....

....

....

....

I enclose 50¢ additional per order to cover handling and postage on all orders under $5.00 (California residents please add 6% sales tax).

Enclosed is $............. ( ) cash, ( ) check, ( ) money order payment in full for all books ordered above (sorry no C.O.D.'s). ( ) I am over 21.

Name ....

Address..

City.............. State...... Zip Code......